SCOTT FORESMA

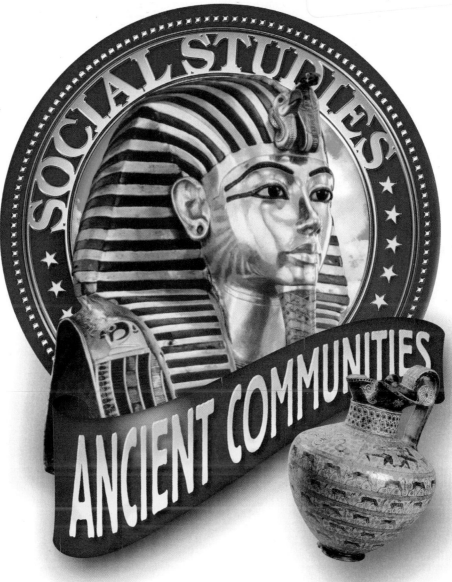

SOCIAL STUDIES

ANCIENT COMMUNITIES

PEARSON

Scott
Foresman

Editorial Offices: Glenview, Illinois • Parsippany, New Jersey • New York, New York
Sales Offices: Parsippany, New Jersey • Duluth, Georgia • Glenview, Illinois •
Coppell, Texas • Ontario, California • Mesa, Arizona

www.sfsocialstudies.com

REVIEWERS

Jackie Olaniel
Wesley Matthews Elementary School
Miami, Florida

Mrs. Toi K. Scott
Wesley Matthews Elementary School
Miami, Florida

Cover page images
Top border, left to right: Greek spinning top, porcelain flask, Emperor Trajan, Egyptian necklace with vulture pendant, replica of Sutton Hoo Helmet, Yoruba grass cloth beaded crown
Center image: Tutankhamen
Center image: Greek vase
Purple background image: Rosetta Stone

ISBN: 0-328-08637-1

2 3 4 5 6 7 8 9 10 V042 13 12 11 10 09 08 07 06 05

Contents

Contents

Contents

Learning New Words

Sometimes when you are reading you find words that are new to you. Here are some tips to help you learn new words.

Before You Read

TIP Look for **highlighted** words. These words are important to understanding the lesson. Here is an example from Unit 1.

A **desert** is a dry area with few plants and animals.

TIP **Look at the new word.**
- Are there parts of the word you already know?
- Have you seen this word before?

While You Read

TIP **Look at the words around the new word.**
- The other words in a sentence can help you decide the meaning of a new word.

TIP **Write down the new word.**

- Write the new word in your Word Journal.
- Use resources such as your teacher or a dictionary to help you learn the meaning of the new word.
- Write down the meaning of the word.

After You Read

TIP **Use the word**

- Write your own sentence using the new word.
- Share your new words with your friends and family.
- Try to make a sentence that uses several of the new words you have learned.

This world map shows the locations of six ancient, or very old, civilizations. A **civilization** is an advanced way of life that usually includes towns, written forms of language, and special kinds of work. You will learn about ancient communities in this book. Today we consider many of these communities part of great civilizations. Each of these civilizations existed at different times in history. Each civilization was located in a different part of the world.

Every ancient civilization is remembered for its achievements. Some were known for their explorers, traders, or inventors. Others created laws and governments that changed the way people lived. The time line at the bottom of these pages shows some major achievements of different ancient civilizations. Read on to learn more about these civilizations and their communities.

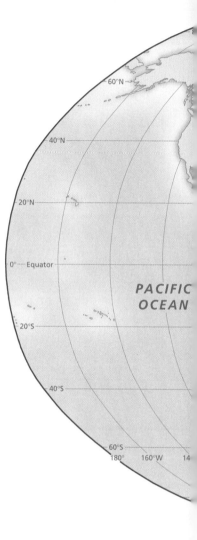

Ancient Civilizations Time Line

5000 B.C.
First people begin settling along Egypt's Nile River.

5000 B.C.
Farming begins along China's Huang He, or Yellow River.

2772 B.C.
The Egyptians make a 365-day calendar.

2600 B.C.
The Egyptians begin building the pyramids at Giza.

1700 B.C.
The Chinese begin using written language.

| 5000 B.C. | 4000 B.C. | 3000 B.C. | 2000 B.C. |

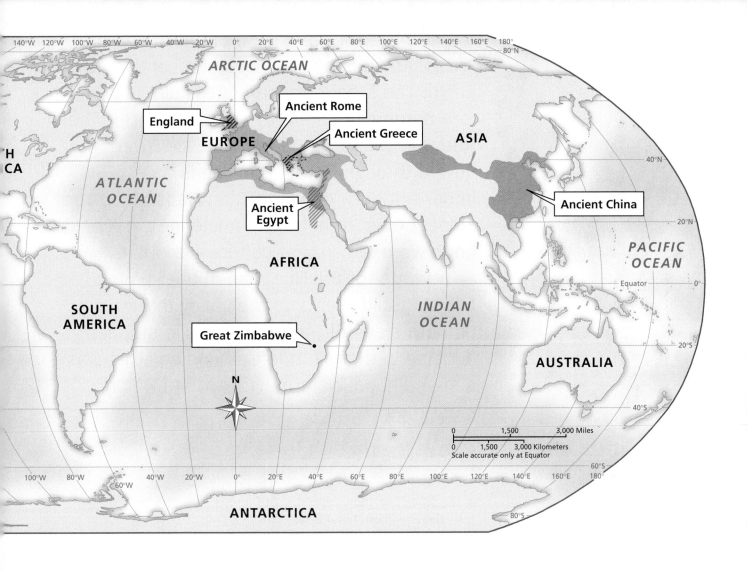

ARCTIC OCEAN

EUROPE

England

Ancient Rome

Ancient Greece

ASIA

Ancient China

ATLANTIC OCEAN

Ancient Egypt

AFRICA

PACIFIC OCEAN

Equator

INDIAN OCEAN

SOUTH AMERICA

Great Zimbabwe

N

AUSTRALIA

0   1,500   3,000 Miles
0   1,500   3,000 Kilometers
Scale accurate only at Equator

ANTARCTICA

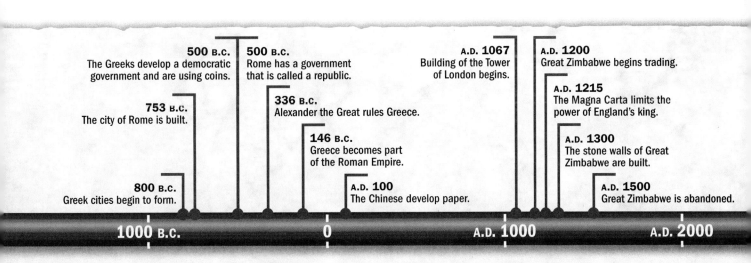

500 B.C.
The Greeks develop a democratic government and are using coins.

500 B.C.
Rome has a government that is called a republic.

A.D. 1067
Building of the Tower of London begins.

A.D. 1200
Great Zimbabwe begins trading.

753 B.C.
The city of Rome is built.

336 B.C.
Alexander the Great rules Greece.

A.D. 1215
The Magna Carta limits the power of England's king.

146 B.C.
Greece becomes part of the Roman Empire.

A.D. 1300
The stone walls of Great Zimbabwe are built.

800 B.C.
Greek cities begin to form.

A.D. 100
The Chinese develop paper.

A.D. 1500
Great Zimbabwe is abandoned.

1000 B.C.   **0**   **A.D. 1000**   **A.D. 2000**

Ancient Egypt

Ancient Egypt was located in northeastern Africa. Africa is one of the seven continents on Earth. The Mediterranean (med I terr A ne an) Sea bordered ancient Egypt to the north. The Red Sea was to the east. The Nile River flowed through Egypt. The Nile is a very important body of water. The Nile is also the longest river in the world. Ancient Egypt could not have been a great culture without it.

The water of the Nile rose in the summer. It would spill over onto the valley that was on both sides of the river. The Nile stopped flooding in the fall. It left behind soil that was rich and good for farming. Farmers would plant their crops in the rich soil.

▶ This map is in an ancient Egyptian earring.

▶ The Nile River flows about 4,000 miles to the Mediterranean Sea.

Much of ancient Egypt was made up of desert. A **desert** is a hot, dry area. The Egyptian deserts had sand, mountains, and cliffs. The ancient Egyptians built underground mines in the desert. They wanted the valuable stones and metals, such as turquoise and gold, that were in the mines. The stones and metals were natural resources. **Natural resources** are things in nature that people can use. The Nile River itself was an important natural resource.

REVIEW Why was the soil of the Nile River Valley good for farming? **Draw Conclusions**

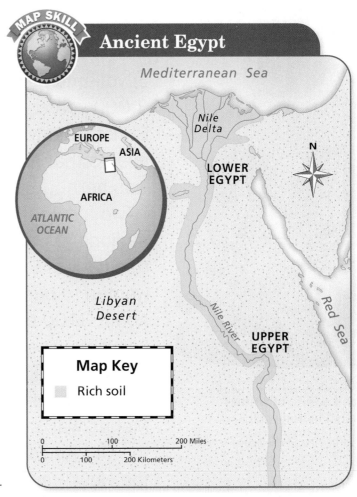

Ancient Egypt

Mediterranean Sea

Nile Delta

EUROPE

ASIA

AFRICA

ATLANTIC OCEAN

N

LOWER EGYPT

Libyan Desert

Nile River

Red Sea

UPPER EGYPT

Map Key

Rich soil

0   100   200 Miles

0   100   200 Kilometers

▶ The Nile River Valley is divided into Lower Egypt and Upper Egypt. Northern Egypt is called Lower Egypt because the land there is lower than the land in southern Egypt.

MAP SKILL Use a Map Scale *About how many miles wide is the Nile Delta?*

History of Ancient Egypt

The civilization of ancient Egypt began about 7,000 years ago, or 5000 B.C. The ancient Egyptian civilization lasted for more than 3,000 years. The term *B.C.* means "Before Christ." Many history books use *B.C.* to show events that happened before Jesus Christ was born.

Two kings ruled ancient Egypt in the beginning. One ruled Upper Egypt. One ruled Lower Egypt. King Menes (MEE nees) wanted to bring together both kingdoms. About 3100 B.C., he led an army into Lower Egypt. He then became the first **pharaoh** (FAIR oh), or king, of ancient Egypt.

Later, the history of ancient Egypt after King Menes was separated into three periods: the Old Kingdom, the Middle Kingdom, and the New Kingdom. During the Old Kingdom, **scribes,** or professional writers, began to write down what happened.

REVIEW When did ancient Egyptian civilization begin? **Main Idea and Details**

▶ Scribes in ancient Egypt used a form of writing called hieroglyphics.

History of Ancient Egypt

About 5000 B.C.
The first people settle along the Nile River.

About 3100 B.C.
King Menes brings together Upper and Lower Egypt. Egyptian pharaohs begin to wear a double crown. The white part stood for Upper Egypt. The red stood for Lower Egypt.

About 3000 B.C.
A 365-day calendar is invented.

| 5000 B.C. | 4500 B.C. | 3500 B.C. | 3000 B.C. |

Egyptian Writing

Ancient Egyptian scribes wrote in hieroglyphics (HI roh GLIF ix), or carved letters. This form of writing was similar to cuneiform (kyoo NEE uh form), or picture writing. Pictures are used in place of words in picture writing. A civilization in southwestern Asia also used cuneiform writing.

In later times, people no longer learned how to read hieroglyphics. No one knew how to read them for a long time. In 1799, a French soldier found a black stone near the Nile River. This stone was named the Rosetta Stone. It was carved with three different kinds of writing. One of those was hieroglyphics. People knew the other two kinds of writing. Now they could learn how to read hieroglyphics.

▶ The discovery of the Rosetta Stone helped solve the mystery of ancient Egyptian hieroglyphics.

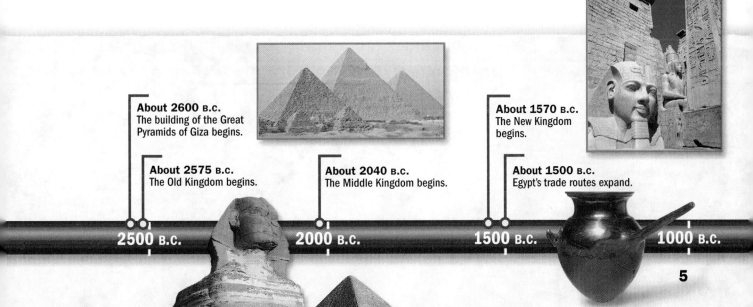

About 2600 B.C.
The building of the Great Pyramids of Giza begins.

About 2575 B.C.
The Old Kingdom begins.

About 2040 B.C.
The Middle Kingdom begins.

About 1570 B.C.
The New Kingdom begins.

About 1500 B.C.
Egypt's trade routes expand.

2500 B.C.   2000 B.C.   1500 B.C.   1000 B.C.

Use Primary and Secondary Sources

What? A **primary source** is created by someone who was there at the time an event happened. That person wrote down thoughts, feelings, or actions. Sometimes that person drew a picture to show what happened. Letters, diaries, paintings, and interviews can be primary sources.

A **secondary source** also tells about something that happened. However, it is written later on, at a different time. The writer or artist might know about later events that will help us to understand earlier events. History books, encyclopedia entries, and newspaper articles can be secondary sources.

Scientist Howard Carter wrote about what it was like to enter the tomb of an Egyptian king. This king's name was Tutankhamun (toot ahng KAH muhn). No one had been in Tutankhamun's tomb for more than 3,000 years. In 1922 Carter found the tomb.

► Tutankhamun became a pharaoh when he was just nine years old.

He wrote:

> *"At first I could see nothing; the hot air escaping from the [room] caused the candle flame to flicker. But . . . as my eyes [got used] to the light, details of the room within [appeared] slowly from the mist— strange animals, [statues], and gold! Everywhere, the [sparkle] of gold!"*

The sentences below tell about the same event. But they are from a history book about Carter's discovery:

> *"Howard Carter spent many years searching for the lost tomb of Tutankhamun. Then one day, his digging uncovered the door of a tomb, and he looked inside. There he found a room full of objects and statues made of gold."*

Why? You can use both primary and secondary sources. You will have a better picture of history if you use both kinds of sources.

How? Use these clues to help figure out if something is a primary or secondary source.

- A writer writes in first person in a primary source. You might read "I thought," "I felt," or "I went" in a primary source. Carter says, "At first I could see nothing."

- A writer writes in third person in a secondary source. You might read "Carter thought," "Carter felt," or "Carter went" in a secondary source.

Think and Apply

❶ Suppose you want to read a story about someone who studied the Nile River. What kind of source would you use?

❷ If you want to read about the history of ancient Egypt, what kind of source might be most helpful? Explain.

❸ In which type of source is the writer also part of the action?

Government of Ancient Egypt

Government is a system for ruling a town, state, or country. Government in ancient Egypt was different than the government Egypt has today. Pharaohs were the leaders of the government. Pharaohs were part of **dynasties** (DY nuh steez), or families of rulers. There were 31 dynasties in ancient Egypt.

The ancient Egyptians thought of the pharaohs as gods. Pharaohs made all of the laws. The ancient Egyptians had to follow these laws. Pharaohs also set up armies to protect the kingdom from people outside of Egypt.

Most pharaohs were men. However, a few pharaohs were women. Some children even became pharaohs. Sometimes an adult had to rule until the child was old enough to be pharaoh.

Pharaohs took a large part of every farmer's crops each year. These crops were used to feed the pharaoh's family and servants. When the Nile River flooded farms, pharaohs kept farmers busy by building government buildings.

The kingdom of ancient Egypt grew over time. Egyptian armies took over kingdoms in other parts of Africa and Southwest Asia.

▶ Queen Hatshepsut (hat shep soot) became pharaoh after her husband died.

▶ This building was built to honor Queen Hatsheput after her death.

Ancient Egypt became an empire during the New Kingdom. An **empire** is a group of countries that are ruled by one ruler or government. Pharaohs came to rule many lands. They built up large armies.

Ancient Egypt eventually grew weak from war. In 332 B.C., it fell to a great civilization in ancient Greece. You will read more about this civilization on pages 30–41.

REVIEW What happened to ancient Egypt during the New Kingdom?
Main Idea and Details

▶ Ramses II, also known as Ramses the Great, was an important pharaoh. He was one of the rulers of ancient Egypt during the New Kingdom.

MAP SKILL
The Egyptian Empire

Mediterranean Sea

Nile Delta

LOWER EGYPT
Giza
Memphis

N

AFRICA

Libyan Desert

Nile River

Red Sea

UPPER EGYPT
Thebes

0   100   200 Miles
0 100 200 Kilometers

Map Key
◼ Old Kingdom
◼ New Kingdom
• City

Nubian Desert

▶ The Egyptians took over African lands to the south and parts of southwest Asia.

MAP SKILL Understand Map Symbols
During which kingdom did the Egyptians control more land?

9

Economy of Ancient Egypt

The ancient Egyptians traded goods with other countries. Why? They had goods and natural resources that other countries did not have. They used the natural resources around them to grow food or make goods. Farmers grew crops such as wheat, beans, and barley. Some craftspeople made wooden furniture. Others made statues out of stone. Jewelers used gold, stones, and glass to make jewelry.

Ancient Egyptians also made linen cloth from the flax plant. Then they made linen into shirts and tunics (TOO nics), which are like loose dresses. A tall grass called **papyrus** (pah PY rus) grows along the Nile River. The ancient Egyptians used papyrus to make baskets, mats, ropes, and sandals.

▶ **The ancient Egyptians pressed reeds of papyrus to make paper.**

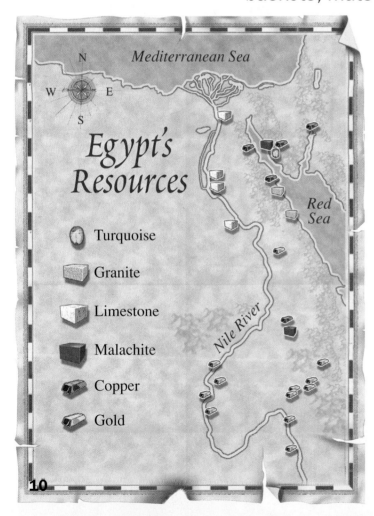

Egypt's Resources

Mediterranean Sea

N W E S

Red Sea

Nile River

- Turquoise
- Granite
- Limestone
- Malachite
- Copper
- Gold

▶ **Granite, gold, and copper were used by ancient Egyptian craftspeople.**

▶ **Copper**

▶ **Granite**

▶ **Gold**

▶ **Many natural resources along the Nile River and the Red Sea helped make Egypt rich.**

Papyrus plants were tied together to make boats. One of the most important uses of papyrus was for making paper.

The ancient Egyptians traded grain, linen cloth, gold, ivory, and papyrus with other countries. Other countries traded wood, spices, silver, and copper in return. Cotton was not an important crop in ancient Egypt. However, today the modern country of Egypt is one of the top countries in the world that **produces,** or grows, cotton.

Ancient Egyptian **merchants,** or traders, had different trade routes. They **transported,** or moved from one place to another, goods along the Nile River. They also traveled across the deserts to reach southern Africa. Merchants brought back goods to the pharaohs. Trade made ancient Egypt's economy grow. Ancient Egypt became very wealthy.

Building **pyramids,** or large buildings that have four walls shaped like triangles, took many natural and human resources. Human resources are workers. You will read more about pyramids on pages 12–13.

▶ Papyrus grass grows along the Nile River.

REVIEW How did trade affect ancient Egypt's economy? **Cause and Effect**

▶ Ivory was used for many items in the pharaoh's palace, including bowls and spoons.

Culture of Ancient Egypt

Ancient Egypt had a rich culture. **Artifacts,** or objects made by people long ago, tell us much about the daily lives of the ancient Egyptians. Probably the biggest artifacts the ancient Egyptians left behind are pyramids! Pyramids are **tombs** (TOOMS), or burial places, for dead pharaohs or wealthy people.

The ancient Egyptians believed that life after death was similar to life on Earth. They built pyramids as houses for the dead. They buried food, jewelry, and statues in the pyramids. This way, they believed, the dead would have these items in their next life. The ancient Egyptians also found a way to preserve or protect the bodies of the dead. They wrapped the bodies in strips of cloth. The wrapped bodies are called mummies.

▶ This wooden board game was played by many ancient Egyptians.

▶ The pictures show some steps the ancient Egyptians used to preserve the bodies of the dead.

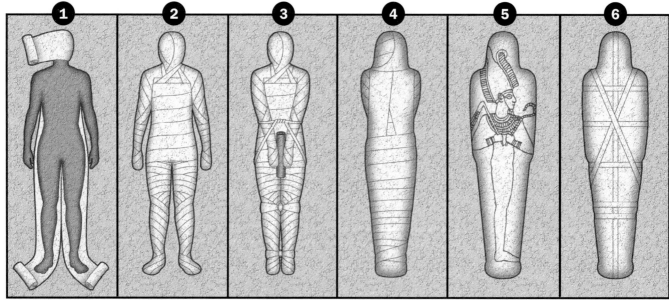

1. The head and neck were wrapped with strips of linen.

2. The arms and legs were wrapped with linen.

3. Legs and arms were tied together and a papyrus scroll was put between the hands.

4. The body was wrapped with more linen.

5. The body was wrapped with cloth. The god Osiris was painted on the cloth.

6. The mummy was wrapped with cloth. Linen attached the cloth to the mummy.

However, what was life like if you were not wealthy or a pharaoh? Most people were farmers and pyramid builders. Some were **craftspeople,** or people who make things. Others were merchants or scribes. Both men and women worked in the fields growing crops.

Ancient Egyptian children played games and helped their parents in the fields. Some had pets such as dogs, cats, or ducks. Fathers taught their young sons a craft such as metalworking. Mothers taught girls how to do jobs at home. Some boys went to school to learn how to read and write.

▶ **Pyramid builders**

REVIEW What was daily life like in ancient Egypt? **Summarize**

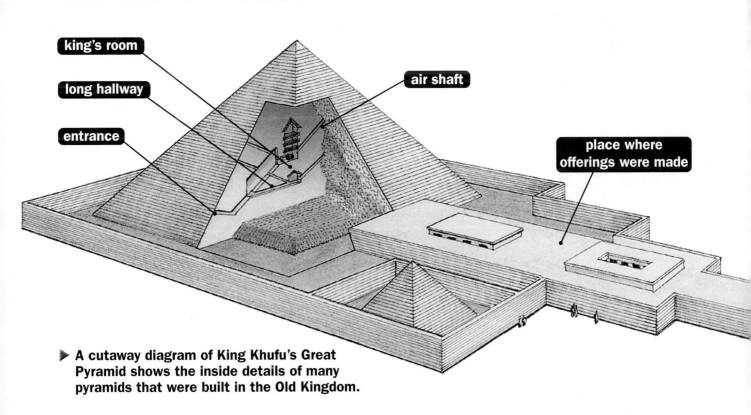

king's room

long hallway

entrance

air shaft

place where offerings were made

▶ **A cutaway diagram of King Khufu's Great Pyramid shows the inside details of many pyramids that were built in the Old Kingdom.**

1. Use each pair of words shown below in a sentence.

pyramid, pharaoh
scribe, papyrus

2. Explain how the deserts were important to the ancient Egyptians.

3. What did scribes in ancient Egypt use to keep written records?

4. Describe ancient Egypt's system of government.

5. What interests you the most about ancient Egypt's culture?

Link to   **Writing**

READ THINK EXPLAIN **Writing Prompt:** Suppose you were an ancient Egyptian who worked on building the Great Pyramid of Giza. Write a letter to a friend describing your experience.

Test Talk

Locate Key Words in the Question.

Directions: Finding key words can help you understand a question. Follow these steps.

- Read the question.
- Look for and circle key words in the question.
- Turn the question into a statement: "I need to find out _____ ."

Try It Write each question on a separate sheet of paper. Circle key words. Choose the correct answer for question 1. Then complete the unfinished sentences.

1. What crops did farmers grow in ancient Egypt?
- **A.** gold, stones, and glass
- **B.** wheat, beans, and barley
- **C.** baskets, mats, and ropes
- **D.** grain, linen, and cloth

I need to find out _____ .

2. What was life like for children in ancient Egypt? Use details from the text to support your answer.

I need to find out _____ .

3. Why were pyramids important to the ancient Egyptians? Use details from the text to support your answer.

I need to find out _____ .

Here are some projects to do in a group or on your own.

Ancient Egyptian Kings and Queens

Learn from biographies Find out more about an ancient Egyptian king or queen. Use primary or secondary sources at the library or on the Internet. When did he or she rule in ancient Egypt? How long did the rule last? What were some things that happened during his or her rule? Write a paragraph using the information you find.

Picture Writing

Create your own hieroglyphics Form a group. Have each group draw a list of picture symbols that stand for letters or words. Then, as a group, write a sentence or short paragraph using everyone's picture language. Trade papers with other groups and see if you can understand other groups' picture writing.

Ancient China

Ancient China was located on the continent of Asia. Today, China is one of the largest countries in Asia. Mountains and deserts surround most of it. These landforms kept people from Europe, Africa, and western Asia from entering China. The Pacific Ocean is the eastern boundary of China. People of ancient China used camels to travel over land and used boats to travel across oceans and up rivers.

Ancient Chinese farmers grew millet, a kind of grain. They grew it along the banks of the Huang He (HWAHNG huh), or Yellow River, in the north. Farmers who lived along the Yangtze (YANG see) River grew rice.

▶ A silk tassel

▶ The Himalaya Mountains are some of the highest mountains in the world.

The Yangtze River is in the south. The weather is warmer there.

The ancient Chinese built their homes and towns high above the rivers. The Yellow River flooded the land every year. These floods were strong enough to wash away the farmers' fields. Farmers would build levees to hold back the river. A **levee** is a wall that is built to stop a river from flooding.

REVIEW What did ancient Chinese farmers do to stop their fields from flooding? **Main Idea and Details**

▶ **Chinese building levees**

▶ **The Great Wall was built to keep out invaders. Over time, Chinese rulers have added on to or rebuilt the Great Wall.**

Compare Maps

What? Maps can give us many kinds of information. Some maps show the borders of countries. Look at the map of ancient China below. It shows borders and rivers of the Han (HAHN) empire. This was an ancient Chinese empire.

Why? Use the maps on these two pages to find the names of the modern countries that were once part of the Han empire. The map on this page shows information about the past. The map on page 19 shows the present-day borders of countries in Asia.

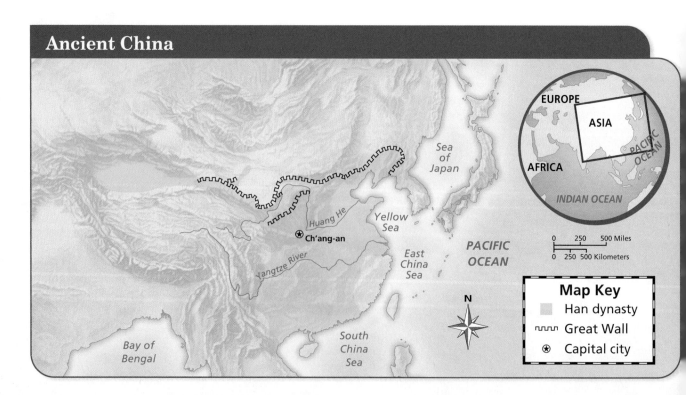

Ancient China

Sea of Japan

EUROPE

ASIA

AFRICA

PACIFIC OCEAN

INDIAN OCEAN

Huang He

Yellow Sea

Ch'ang-an

Yangtze River

East China Sea

PACIFIC OCEAN

0   250   500 Miles
0 250 500 Kilometers

N

Bay of Bengal

South China Sea

Map Key
Han dynasty
Great Wall
Capital city

How? First, find some details that are on both maps. For example, look for the Yangtze River or the Huang He on the map of ancient China. Then find the same river on the second map. This will help you locate the same area of land on both maps. Next, trace the shape of the Han empire on a separate piece of paper. Place your tracing over the second map. This will tell you what present-day countries were once part of the Han empire.

Think and Apply

❶ Why is it helpful to compare maps?

❷ Compare the two maps. Was the capital of ancient China in the same location as the capital of China is today?

❸ On which map is China's land area larger? Was China larger during the Han empire, or is it larger today?

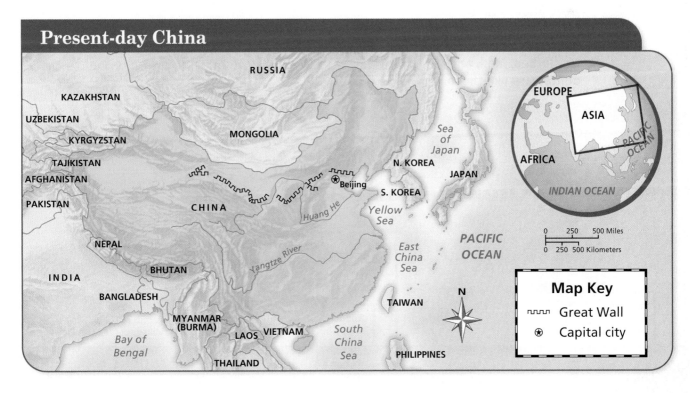

Present-day China

RUSSIA

KAZAKHSTAN

UZBEKISTAN

KYRGYZSTAN

MONGOLIA

Sea of Japan

TAJIKISTAN

N. KOREA

JAPAN

AFGHANISTAN

Beijing

S. KOREA

PAKISTAN

CHINA

Huang He

Yellow Sea

NEPAL

Yangtze River

East China Sea

PACIFIC OCEAN

BHUTAN

INDIA

BANGLADESH

TAIWAN

N

MYANMAR (BURMA)

LAOS VIETNAM

South China Sea

Bay of Bengal

PHILIPPINES

THAILAND

EUROPE

ASIA

AFRICA

PACIFIC OCEAN

INDIAN OCEAN

0   250   500 Miles
0   250 500 Kilometers

Map Key

⌐⌐⌐ Great Wall

✷ Capital city

History of Ancient China

Ancient China was ruled by dynasties for thousands of years, just like ancient Egypt. The earliest known Chinese dynasty was called the Shang dynasty. This dynasty ruled China for more than 600 years.

Writing in China began as carved symbols during the Shang dynasty. Over time, these early symbols formed into the characters the Chinese write with today. There are thousands of symbols in the Chinese written language. Writing in ancient China was a special skill. It took years to learn how to write.

▶ Tombs of Chinese emperors were filled with items they believed they would need in their next lives, such as clothes, food, and containers like these.

History of Ancient China

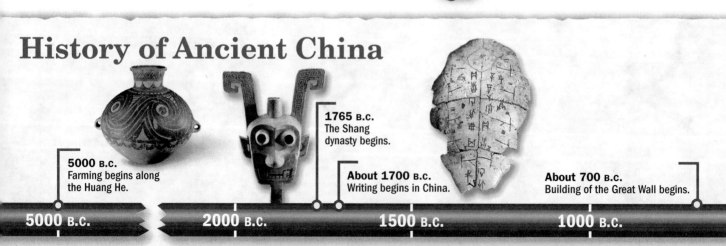

5000 B.C.
Farming begins along the Huang He.

1765 B.C.
The Shang dynasty begins.

About 1700 B.C.
Writing begins in China.

About 700 B.C.
Building of the Great Wall begins.

5000 B.C.   2000 B.C.   1500 B.C.   1000 B.C.

Much of what we know about ancient Chinese history comes from one history book. The writer of the book was Sima Qian (SEE ma CHEE en). Sima Qian lived during the Han dynasty. The book tells about history up to the Han dynasty. Each chapter of the book tells about a different part of ancient Chinese life. One chapter tells about kings and emperors. Another chapter tells about important ideas of the time. Sima Qian's book was so complete that for a long time all Chinese history books followed its style.

▶ **Sima Qian**

REVIEW How was ancient China ruled? How do we know? **Summarize**

▶ Early Chinese writing used pictures of people, animals, and objects. These symbols look a lot like the characters used in Chinese writing today.

206 B.C.
The Han dynasty begins.

221 B.C.
Qin Shi Huangdi becomes the first emperor of China.

About A.D. 100
Paper is invented in ancient China.

| 500 B.C. | A.D. 1 | A.D. 500 | A.D. 1000 |

Government of Ancient China

▶ Shi Huangdi was emperor of ancient China from 221 B.C. to 210 B.C.

In ancient China the king was the head of the government. The nobles were next in importance. **Nobles** were men who could own their own land. Farmers and other workers could not own land. Only nobles could have government jobs.

Ancient China was made up of seven different states, or kingdoms. These kingdoms fought with each other all the time. Then the kingdom of Qin (CHIN) won control of all the kingdoms. Shi Huangdi (SHEE HWONG dee), who was the king of Qin, became the first emperor of China. An **emperor** is the ruler of an empire.

Shi Huangdi built roads and canals to connect all parts of his empire. He also made sure that only one form of writing was used throughout his empire. Each separate kingdom had used its own way of writing at that time. Shi Huangdi chose the easiest writing system. Then all Chinese people could understand each other.

New rulers took control of ancient China about 2,200 years ago. This was the start of the Han dynasty. The Han emperors ruled fairly. They had schools built to teach people how to do government jobs. Now the nobles could no longer be the only people to have these jobs.

REVIEW How did rule by the Han dynasty affect the government of ancient China? **Cause and Effect**

▶ Shi Huangdi had an army of about 6,000 life-sized soldiers built for his tomb. The soldiers were made out of terra cotta, a type of clay.

Economy of Ancient China

Silk was an important product in ancient China. Silk comes from silkworms, which are a kind of caterpillar. Silkworms eat leaves from mulberry trees. Then they spin cocoons as they grow. A cocoon is like a bag that some insects spin around themselves. It protects them while they grow. First, the ancient Chinese pulled apart the silkworm cocoons. Next, the strings of the cocoon were spun into thread. Finally, the Chinese wove the thread into silk cloth.

Silk was made and used only in China for hundreds of years. Then Chinese traders began to sell silk across Asia. Silk was carried by camel caravans along a trade route called the Silk Road. A **caravan** is a group of people and animals that travel together.

▶ The ancient Chinese used the cocoon of the silkworm to create thread. The thread was used to make cloth.

▶ Marco Polo might have traveled from Italy in Europe to China in Asia along the Silk Road. He left his home in A.D. 1271. His books taught Europeans a lot about China.

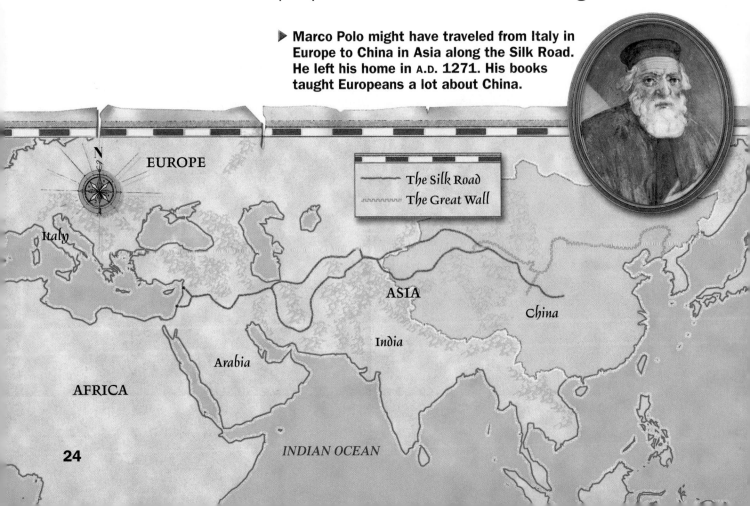

N

EUROPE

The Silk Road
The Great Wall

Italy

ASIA

China

India

Arabia

AFRICA

INDIAN OCEAN

The Silk Road stretched from China all the way to the Mediterranean Sea. Merchants also carried spices, tea, and porcelain along this route. The silk trade brought great wealth to ancient China.

At first, ancient Chinese merchants traded their goods for other goods. Then ancient China began to use money within the empire. Chinese coins were made of copper. When Shi Huangdi became emperor, he had his own coins designed. He wanted the entire empire to use the same money.

▶ The ancient Chinese used copper coins for money.

REVIEW How did the Silk Road affect ancient China's economy? **Draw Conclusions**

FACT FILE

Paper Making

Paper was invented in ancient China about 1,900 years ago. The first paper was made of silk waste. Later, the Chinese used a mixture of tree bark, plants, and rags to make paper. First, they dried this mixture on screens made of bamboo, a kind of grass. Next, the paper was lifted off the bamboo screen.

The ancient Chinese used paper for writing and drawing. Over time, it was even used to make money. Soon, people began to use paper in other parts of Asia and the rest of the world.

▶ A screen is used to lift the paper mixture from the water.

Culture of Ancient China

Most ancient Chinese were farmers. They lived in small villages. Everyone in the family helped grow and harvest the crops. Farmers also had pigs and chickens. Their houses were made of wood and mud.

Family was the most important part of ancient Chinese culture. Families were often made up of many generations living together in the same home. A **generation** is all the people in a family who are about the same age. The oldest man was in charge of everyone in the household.

In ancient China parents taught their children. Boys learned how to farm. Girls learned household jobs such as cooking and sewing. Children still had some time to play games such as puzzles and cards. They also liked outdoor ball games. Adults had little free time. But they enjoyed playing card games and board games.

▶ Most people in ancient China wore clothing made of plant fibers. The richest people wore clothing made of silk.

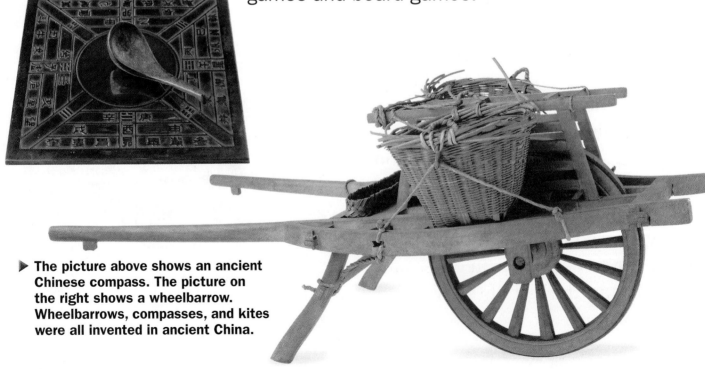

▶ The picture above shows an ancient Chinese compass. The picture on the right shows a wheelbarrow. Wheelbarrows, compasses, and kites were all invented in ancient China.

Since ancient times, the dragon has been an important symbol to the Chinese. The Chinese believe that dragons mean good luck. They celebrate each New Year with a dragon dance. People wear dragon costumes and dance to the music of drums and gongs. This **tradition,** or custom, started in ancient times.

REVIEW How was ancient China's culture like that of ancient Egypt? How was it different? **Compare and Contrast**

▶ Ancient Chinese rulers wore silk robes with dragons pictured on them.

▶ Dragons are often found in Chinese pottery, art, poetry, and songs.

▶ Dragon in a Chinese New Year parade

27

Review

1. Write one or two sentences describing the difference between a noble and an emperor.

2. How did the geography of China keep people from other countries away for hundreds of years?

3. Why was paper an important invention in ancient China?

4. How did the Silk Road get its name?

5. Why did the use of coins in ancient China make trade easier?

Link to Writing

READ THINK EXPLAIN **Writing Prompt:** Shi Huangdi introduced one writing system for all of China. Think about how this helped to bring together all the kingdoms in the country. Write about other things that might help connect people in a country.

 **Test Talk**

Locate Key Words in the Text

Directions: Think about where you need to look for an answer. Follow these steps.

- Read the question.
- Look for and circle key words in the question.
- Look for and circle key words in the text that match the key words in the question.
- Decide where to look for the answer.
  — You may have to **look in one place in the text.**
  — You may have to **look in several places in the text.**
  — You may have to **combine what you know with what the author tells you.**

Try It Write each question and answer on a separate piece of paper. Circle key words. Complete the unfinished sentences.

1. Much of what we know about ancient Chinese history comes from one book. Who wrote it?
   - **A.** Shi Huangdi
   - **B.** Marco Polo
   - **C.** Huang He
   - **D.** Sima Qian

   I found the answer in _____ .

2. Which of these is an important symbol to the Chinese?
   - **A.** millet
   - **B.** copper
   - **C.** dragon
   - **D.** silk

   I found the answer in _____ .

3. Explain how the ancient Chinese made silk.

   I found the answer in _____ .

Here are some projects to do in a group or on your own.

Learn about Land and Water

Draw a map Form a group. Find a physical map of China. Make sure that the map key shows such features as mountains, rivers, and deserts. Working with your group, draw a map that shows where the major mountains, rivers, and deserts in China are located. Use a different color for each feature.

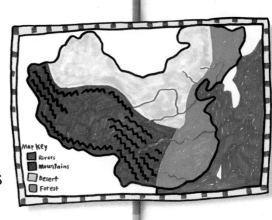

Made in China

Create a poster Research one ancient Chinese invention. Then make a poster showing this invention. Label the parts of the invention to show what the object was made of and how it was made. Present your poster to the class.

Ancient Greece

Ancient Greece was located in southeastern Europe along the eastern end of the Mediterranean Sea. Most of its land was a peninsula. A **peninsula** is land that has water around three sides of it. Ancient Greece also had more than 400 islands. These islands and the Greek peninsula make up much of the modern country of Greece today.

The weather in ancient Greece made farming hard. The summers were hot and dry. The winters were very wet. Farmers raised only those crops and animals that could survive in this climate.

▶ **A statue of Atlas**

MAP SKILL

The Greek Peninsula and Islands

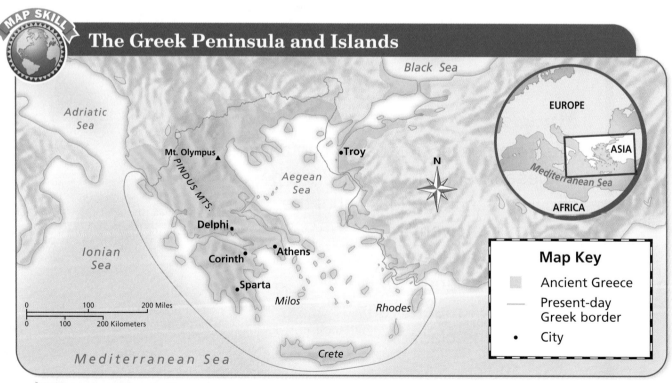

Black Sea

Adriatic Sea

Mt. Olympus ▲

PINDUS MTS.

•Troy

Aegean Sea

N

EUROPE

ASIA

Mediterranean Sea

AFRICA

Delphi •

Ionian Sea

Corinth •

•Athens

• Sparta

Milos

Rhodes

| 0 | 100 | 200 Miles |
| 0 | 100 | 200 Kilometers |

Mediterranean Sea

Crete

Map Key

▪ Ancient Greece

— Present-day Greek border

• City

▶ **Greece is made up of a peninsula and many islands.**

MAP SKILL   Understand Cardinal Directions   *Is Mt. Olympus north or south of Athens?*

Olives and grapes grew well in Greece's rocky areas during the long, hot summers. Animals such as sheep and goats could live in the dry climate.

Ancient Greece was very hilly. This made travel by land difficult. Most communities were built close to the coast and on the many islands. This was so that people could travel on the water. Sailing was an important part of life. Ships were faster and carried more than wagons could.

REVIEW How did the climate of ancient Greece affect the crops that farmers grew? **Main Idea and Details**

▶ Most of Greece has mountains. The Pindus Mountains stretch from north to south through the center of Greece.

▶ The Mediterranean Sea links all of the islands in Greece. It connected the ancient Greeks to other cultures.

History of Ancient Greece

The ancient Greeks began to trade about 2,800 years ago. They traded crops and pottery for goods from other lands. This made them richer. Their culture then began to spread. The ancient Greeks built a large and powerful civilization over time. This period is known as the Classical Period. Athens and Sparta were two important Greek cities that formed during this time.

The kingdom of Macedonia was located just north of ancient Greece. When Philip II was king of Macedonia, he invaded Greece with his powerful army. He took over the whole country. His son, Alexander, became king a few years later. Alexander traveled more than 20,000 miles with his army. He took over many lands. Alexander ruled the largest empire in the ancient world for about 15 years. Because of this, he is known today as Alexander the Great. Alexander's empire brought Greek customs, literature, and art to the rest of the world.

▶ **Philip II of Macedonia built a great army. His soldiers were very loyal to him.**

The Rise of Ancient Greece

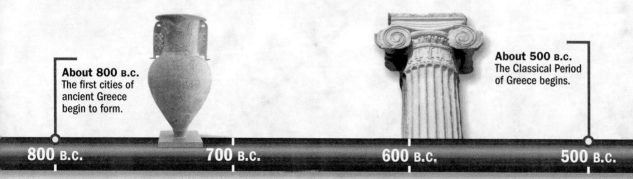

About 800 B.C.
The first cities of ancient Greece begin to form.

About 500 B.C.
The Classical Period of Greece begins.

800 B.C.   700 B.C.   600 B.C.   500 B.C.

Greek influence can be seen throughout Alexander's empire. The ancient Greeks are known for the temples they left behind. They built huge marble temples in their cities. These temples are famous for their rows of columns. The tall columns held up the temples. Greek building styles were copied in cities throughout Alexander's empire.

REVIEW What happened after Alexander became king? **Sequence**

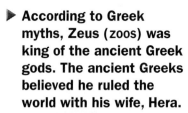

▶ According to Greek myths, Zeus (zoos) was king of the ancient Greek gods. The ancient Greeks believed he ruled the world with his wife, Hera.

FACT FILE

Greek Myths

The ancient Greeks had many beliefs. They thought that gods and goddesses controlled everything. They told stories called myths to explain events in nature. Gods and goddesses were often characters in these myths. The ancient Greeks believed their gods lived on Mount Olympus. From this mountain the gods watched over the people. Mount Olympus is the highest mountain in Greece.

▶ **Mount Olympus**

438 B.C.
The Parthenon is completed.

336 B.C.
Alexander rules ancient Greece and begins to build an empire.

400 B.C.   **300 B.C.**   **200 B.C.**   **100 B.C.**

Government of Ancient Greece

Ancient Greece was first made up of many small communities. The mountains and islands kept them apart from each other. Later, some of these communities grew into city-states. A **city-state** was made up of a city and the farmland around it. Each city-state had its own laws, courts, and money. Many also had an acropolis, or a "city at the top." Government buildings and temples usually were located on the acropolis.

The richest men in the community first ruled the city-states. But by 500 B.C., Athens had become a democracy. **Democracy** means

▶ One way citizens of ancient Athens voted was to use an ostraka (OS-TRAH-ka).

▶ The Parthenon was an important building at the top of the Acropolis in Athens.

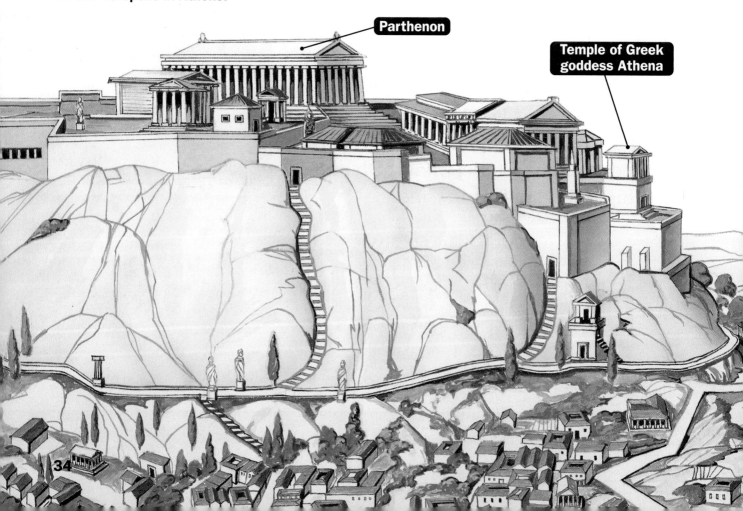

Parthenon

Temple of Greek goddess Athena

"rule by the people." People vote for their leaders in a democracy. Only men could vote in ancient Athens.

At first, any man born in Athens was considered a citizen. A **citizen** is a person who has rights and responsibilities in a community. Later on, a person could only be a citizen if both parents had been born in Athens. Athenian citizens met each month. They talked about and voted on laws. These laws helped the city.

► This statue shows a Greek woman cooking.

REVIEW How was the government of ancient Greece like our government today? How was it different? **Compare and Contrast**

► The Parthenon in Athens was built between 447 B.C. and 432 B.C.

► The Areopagus (AR ee OP uh gus) in Athens was a place where important leaders in ancient Greece met.

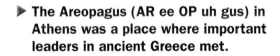

Areopagus

Use a Bar Graph

What? A bar graph uses bars to show how things relate to one another. It can help you compare amounts or numbers. Look at the bar graph below. It shows the average temperature in Athens, Greece, in a year. Each of the months shown has its own bar.

Why? The climate of ancient Greece affected Greek culture. Temperature is an important part of climate. Some months of the year are warmer than other months. Warmer months are usually better for growing crops. You can use a bar graph to compare temperatures in different months or cities.

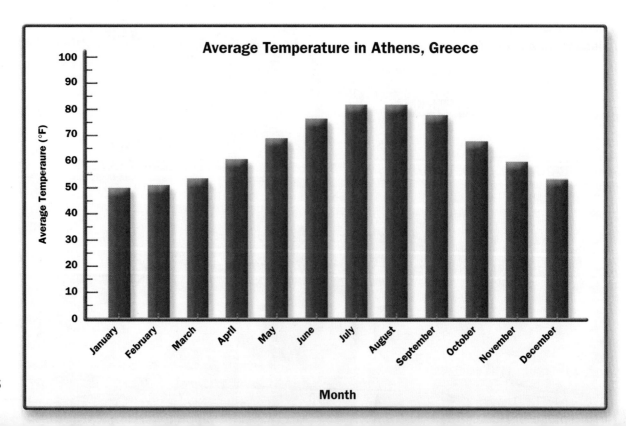

Average Temperature in Athens, Greece

How? First, look at the title of the bar graph. The title tells you what information the graph shows. Next, look at the words and numbers along the left side and at the bottom of the graph. They tell you what is being measured. They also tell you how it is being measured. Each bar on the graph shows the average monthly temperature in Athens, Greece. You can see which is the coldest month and which is the warmest month.

Economy of Ancient Greece

Ancient Greece had few natural resources. However, its location on the Mediterranean Sea made it easy for Greece to trade with other lands. Ancient Greece's most important crops for trade were grapes and olives. The ancient Greeks also traded painted vases and other pottery. They traded these items for goods such as iron, marble, and wood. Iron was made into tools. Marble was made into statues. Wood was used to build houses and ships.

▶ The ancient Greeks began to use coins about 2,700 years ago. This made trade with people from different lands easier.

▶ The agora in ancient Athens grew and changed over time. This is how the agora may have looked in 4 B.C.

Great Stoa
A stoa was a building with shops and meeting places.

Temple of Dionysus
Dionysus was a Greek god.

Alexander's empire connected cities in ancient Greece to cities in Egypt and parts of Asia. This meant that there were more people with whom to trade.

The centers of trade in ancient Greek cities were called agoras. An **agora** (uh GO ruh) was an open marketplace in the middle of each important city. Public buildings and temples were usually around the agora. The most famous agora was in Athens. People came from all over to exchange goods, money, and new ideas. They also went there to meet friends.

▶ **Grains and olives at a market in Greece**

REVIEW Why was the agora important to the ancient Greeks? **Main Idea and Details**

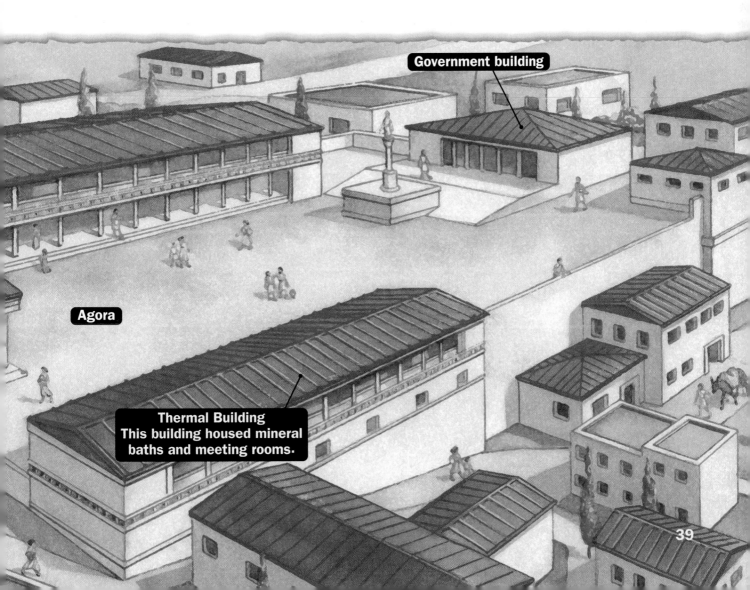

Government building

Agora

Thermal Building
This building housed mineral baths and meeting rooms.

Culture of Ancient Greece

The ancient Greeks were famous for their pottery, sculptures, and statues. They made statues of Greek leaders and athletes. The statues could be found in temples, public places, and people's homes. Painted vases were also very common. They often showed scenes of daily life.

What was daily life like for the ancient Greeks? Most families lived in small houses made of wood, mud bricks, or stones. They cooked their meals outside. They often caught fish in the sea. They also grew grains such as wheat and barley to make bread. Olives were used to make olive oil. This oil was used in cooking. It was also used in lamps and even as body lotion.

Greek children played with toys such as rattles, clay animals, and dolls. Boys started

▶ A spinning top from ancient Greece

▶ A house in ancient Greece

courtyard

well

school at the age of seven. There they were taught reading, writing, math, music, and sports. Girls did not go to school. Instead they helped their mothers at home. They learned to cook and weave cloth.

The ancient Greeks wore light and simple clothing. A rectangular piece of cloth could be used in many different ways. It could be a long robe, a short dress, or even a cape.

Sports were an important part of ancient Greek culture. The most popular competition was the Olympics (oh LIM pix). Many of the Olympic events in ancient Greece were like the ones we see in the modern Olympic Games. These events include running, jumping, boxing, and wrestling.

REVIEW What was daily life like in ancient Greece? **Summarize**

▶ The ancient Greeks used both marble and bronze to make statues.

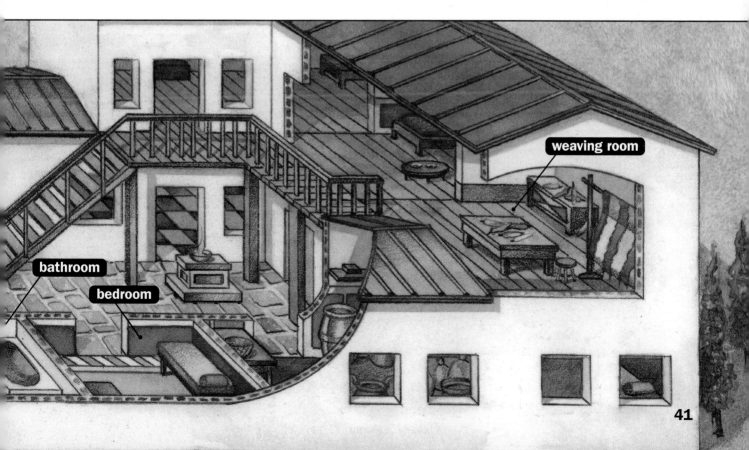

weaving room

bathroom

bedroom

1. What are two ways that life in ancient Greece was different than your life is today?

2. Why did sailing become an important part of life for the ancient Greeks?

3. Describe a city-state.

4. How did the male citizens of Athens participate in their local government?

5. Explain how the culture of ancient Greece spread to other parts of the world.

Link to **Writing**

READ THINK EXPLAIN **Writing Prompt:** The agora was an important meeting place in ancient Greece. Think about the reasons why people met at agoras. Write about the different activities that took place there.

 **Test Talk**

Choose the Right Answer

Directions: Sometimes a question asks you to choose the best answer. Follow these steps.

- Read the question.
- Read each answer choice.
- Cross out answer choices that you know are wrong.
- Mark your answer choice.
- Check your answer. Compare your answer to the text.

Try It Write the answer choices for each question on a separate piece of paper. Cross out choices that you know are wrong. Mark your answer choice. Then check your answer.

1. Ancient Greece was located along which sea?
   - A. Arabian Sea
   - B. Caribbean Sea
   - C. Mediterranean Sea
   - D. Red Sea

2. Where did the ancient Greeks believe their gods lived?
   - A. in Sparta
   - B. on Mount Olympus
   - C. in Macedonia
   - D. in the agora

3. Which members of the community could vote in ancient Athens?
   - A. only men
   - B. only women
   - C. only children
   - D. everyone

Here are some projects to do in a group or on your own.

A Greek Vacation

Make a travel poster In Greece today you can still visit some of the buildings and statues from ancient times. Choose an ancient place in Greece you would like to visit. Find out about it. Make a travel poster advertising the place you researched. Display your poster to the class.

Let's Play!

Become an Olympic Athlete
Choose and research one Olympic sporting event that took place in ancient Greece. First, tell the class about the sporting event. Then, show the class how to play the sport. Use equipment if it will help you show how to play the sport.

Ancient Rome

The city of Rome is located in Italy. Italy is a country in southern Europe. Like Greece, Italy is a peninsula. It extends into the Mediterranean Sea. Italy is shaped like a boot. This shape makes it easy to find on a map. In the northern part of Italy are mountains called the Alps.

At first, Rome was just a small farming village. The farmers grew crops along the Tiber River. They raised sheep and goats on Rome's rolling hills. Then more villages were built. These villages joined together to form the city of Rome.

Rome took over all of the Italian peninsula in the next few hundred years. Rome soon

▶ This map is in the frame of a bronze mirror from ancient Rome.

▶ The Via Appia was a famous Roman road. It is still in use today.

became the center of a huge empire. The empire grew to include thousands of miles across Europe into Africa and Asia.

The Roman civilization was known for their paved roads. These roads allowed the Roman army to travel throughout the empire. Ancient Romans also used the roads to carry goods to lands throughout the empire.

Roman roads began in the city of Rome. They covered more than 50,000 miles. Roman roads were built higher in the middle than on the sides. This let rainwater run off into ditches so that the roads would not flood. Ancient Roman roads were built so well that many are still used today.

▶ Paved roads linked Rome to many other towns. These roads were first built so that armies could get from place to place.

REVIEW How did roads help the Roman Empire? **Draw Conclusions**

45

History of Ancient Rome

According to Roman legend, Rome was named for Romulus (ROM yoo lis). Romulus and Remus (REE mis) were twins. They were the sons of Mars, the Roman god of war. The same legend says that Romulus was the first king of Rome.

The city of Rome had taken over all of Italy by 250 B.C. Then war broke out between the Romans and the people of Carthage in North Africa. Both sides wanted to control trade in the Mediterranean Sea.

The people of Carthage had a special weapon—elephants. They used elephants to scare the Romans. Soldiers also used them for transportation. The war lasted for more than 100 years. Finally, the Romans won. They took over Carthage's lands.

The Romans then began to take over all of the kingdoms around the Mediterranean. They continued to take over more lands during the next 150 years. One of these lands was what we know today as Great Britain.

Julius Caesar (SEE zer) was a general in the Roman army. He came to power after leading

► Around 200 B.C. the Roman army captured more than 100 elephants in a battle with the city of Carthage.

History of Ancient Rome

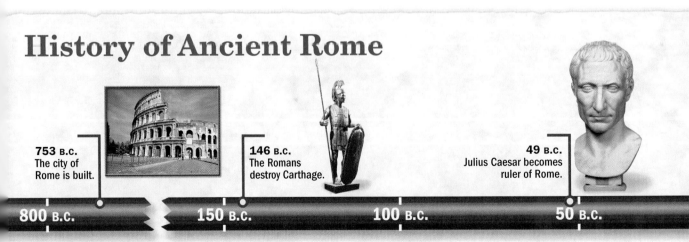

753 B.C.
The city of Rome is built.

146 B.C.
The Romans destroy Carthage.

49 B.C.
Julius Caesar becomes ruler of Rome.

800 B.C.   150 B.C.   100 B.C.   50 B.C.

Roman Empire

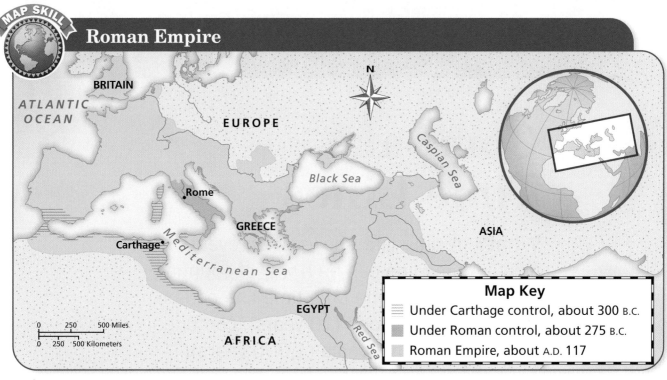

BRITAIN

ATLANTIC OCEAN

EUROPE

N

Caspian Sea

Black Sea

Rome

GREECE

ASIA

Carthage

Mediterranean Sea

EGYPT

Red Sea

AFRICA

0   250   500 Miles
0   250   500 Kilometers

Map Key

≡ Under Carthage control, about 300 B.C.

▨ Under Roman control, about 275 B.C.

☐ Roman Empire, about A.D. 117

▶ By A.D. 117, much of the land in Europe and Northern Africa was part of the Roman Empire.

MAP SKILL   Use a Map   *What body of water separated Rome from Carthage?*

the army in many wars. He was the first **caesar,** or ruler, of Rome. After his death, civil war broke out. Another general in the army wanted to bring peace to Rome. He was given the title *Augustus* (aw GUS tus). Augustus became Rome's first emperor.

REVIEW   How did winning the war against Carthage change the size of Rome? **Cause and Effect**

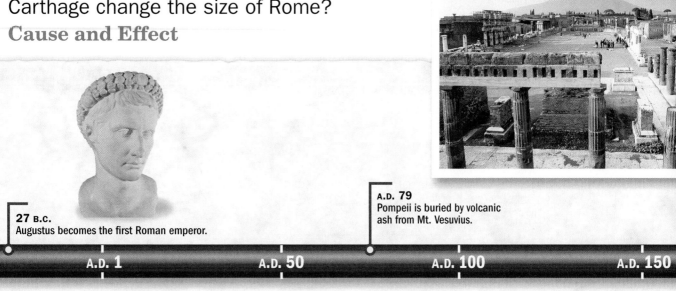

27 B.C.
Augustus becomes the first Roman emperor.

A.D. 79
Pompeii is buried by volcanic ash from Mt. Vesuvius.

A.D. 1   A.D. 50   A.D. 100   A.D. 150

Compare Time Lines

What? A **time line** shows when events took place. A time line can be a way of counting years. Calendar time on a time line can be measured in decades (10 years), centuries (100 years), or millennia (1,000 years).

Why? Time lines can show events and different time periods. They help us understand when things happened. We can see some events on time lines that were happening at the same time in different places. We can also

Events of Ancient Greece

800 B.C.
The first cities of Ancient Greece begin to form.

776 B.C.
The first Olympic Games are held in Greece.

About 500 B.C.
Democracy begins in Athens.

438 B.C.
The Parthenon is completed.

800 B.C.   700 B.C.   600 B.C.   500 B.C.   400 B.C.

Events of Ancient Rome

753 B.C.
The city of Rome is built.

800 B.C.   700 B.C.   600 B.C.   500 B.C.   400 B.C.

see events that were taking place at different times.

How? Study the two time lines on these pages. The titles tell what each one is about. Notice that some events in ancient Greece took place before Rome became a city. You can see that some events in ancient Rome happened after Greece became part of the Roman Empire. You will notice that sections on the time line are broken into centuries, or 100-year periods.

Think and Apply

❶ Name one event that took place at the same time in both ancient Greece and ancient Rome.

❷ Was the city of Rome built before or after the Parthenon was completed?

❸ When you look at both time lines together, which event happened last?

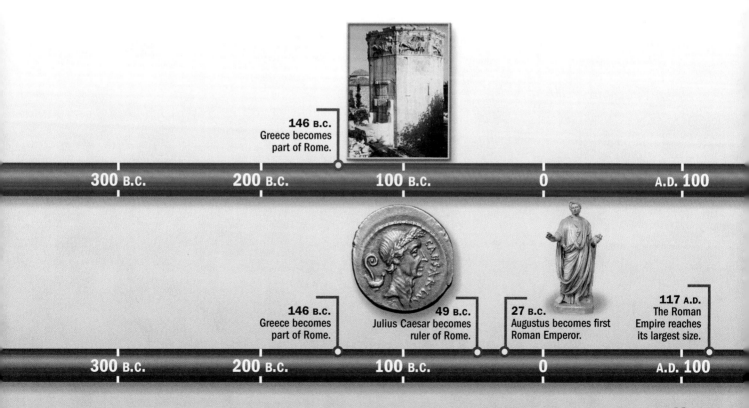

146 B.C.
Greece becomes part of Rome.

300 B.C.   200 B.C.   100 B.C.   0   A.D. 100

146 B.C.
Greece becomes part of Rome.

49 B.C.
Julius Caesar becomes ruler of Rome.

27 B.C.
Augustus becomes first Roman Emperor.

117 A.D.
The Roman Empire reaches its largest size.

300 B.C.   200 B.C.   100 B.C.   0   A.D. 100

Government of Ancient Rome

▶ The two leaders of the Senate had many of the same powers as a king. One usually stayed in Rome and the other led the Roman army.

▶ The Senate created a strong government for the people of Rome. Emperor Augustus had great respect for the members of the Senate.

Kings ruled Rome for its first 250 years. Then the Romans set up a republic. A **republic** is a form of government in which citizens elect people to speak or act for them. The **Senate** (SEN it) ruled the Roman republic. It was a group of men who came from the richest and most powerful Roman families. The Senate helped Rome become an empire.

The Senate made Augustus the first Roman emperor. But then the Senate lost a lot of its power. Roman emperors became more powerful than the Senate. They were often thought of as gods. Some ruled fairly. Others were very strict and even cruel.

The ancient Romans had many ideas about law that we still follow today. They believed

that no one could be found guilty until all the facts were known. They also believed that a person accused of a crime had the right to see a judge.

Much of our country's legal, or law, system is based on ideas from the ancient Romans. The Roman republic has also been a model for the U.S. government. Senators, judges, and juries were all part of ancient Rome's government.

Government was also responsible for supplying fresh water to Roman towns. Water was carried into the towns through aqueducts. **Aqueducts** are systems of pipes for carrying water. They have lasted for hundreds of years.

▶ **The Romans built a system of aqueducts. These aqueducts brought water from the hills to other areas that needed water.**

REVIEW What happened after the Senate made Augustus the first Roman emperor? **Sequence**

Economy of Ancient Rome

Goods such as pottery, grain, wool, and silver were shipped throughout the Roman Empire. The silver was used to make jewelry and money.

Romans traveled along the Silk Road to trade with countries in Asia. Items that were traded included silk, which was used to make clothing for the wealthy, and spices. The Romans used spices such as pepper, ginger, cloves, and cinnamon in their cooking.

Every large Roman town had a forum. Forums were like ancient Greek agoras. The forum was the main marketplace. The ancient Romans went to forums to do banking, trading, and shopping. The forum was also

► The Roman emperor had coins made that were used across the entire empire. This made trade much easier. Coins were made of gold, silver, and bronze.

► Olive oil was usually shipped in large pottery jars. The jars were tightly packed together and carried on ships.

a place where people could make speeches. Forums were sometimes used for festivals and religious ceremonies.

REVIEW Name three items that were traded across the Roman empire.

Main Idea and Details

▶ The forum had theaters, shops, and meeting places. Later, buildings in the forum also included temples to honor the Roman gods.

Mathematics in the Ancient World

Then and Now

The ancient Greeks made important advances in mathematics. Many ideas from the Greek world spread to the Islamic world. People from lands such as Spain and Persia studied ancient Greek mathematics. But they had to have it translated into Arabic. Arabic is the language spoken by many people in southwestern Asia and northern Africa. The numbers that we use today are based on an Arabic number system.

The Romans also created their own system of numbers. This system is known as Roman numerals. The letters M, D, C, L, X, V, and I stood for the numbers 1000, 500, 100, 50, 10, 5, and 1. Numbers could be written by combining these letters.

▶ Roman numerals are still used today. Sometimes they can be found on clocks and watches.

Culture of Ancient Rome

Most people in Rome lived in crowded apartment buildings. Only very rich people had their own homes. These homes were very large, brightly painted houses with gardens. Roman houses were made of stone, mud bricks, or wood. The roofs were made of clay tiles.

Roman houses usually did not have baths. People went to public bathhouses to get clean. They used olive oil instead of soap. People also went to bathhouses to exercise, play ball games, or meet friends.

The family was very important to the ancient Romans. The father was the head of the family. Fathers taught their sons how to read and write. Mothers taught their daughters how to spin, weave, and sew. Later on, wealthy parents sent their sons to schools. Sometimes their daughters went too.

Roman clothes were usually woven by hand at home. The cloth was made of wool or linen. The most common style of clothing was a

▶ Togas were worn by men and women at first. Later, only men wore them.

▶ Many Roman bathhouses had heaters built under the floors.

tunic, just like in ancient Egypt. Important men of ancient Rome wore a heavy white robe called a toga (TOE ga).

The Romans brought their culture to every land in the empire. Everyone in the empire had to follow Roman laws and customs. They also had to worship the Roman gods.

The Romans were the most famous builders of the ancient world. They built marble temples and huge public buildings. Many of their buildings were like those of ancient Greece. Yet the Romans also had their own styles. They invented the dome, which is a round-shaped roof. The Romans were also the first to make concrete. Concrete was stronger and cheaper to use than stone.

REVIEW Describe how family was important to the ancient Romans. Summarize

▶ A festival in honor of Mars, the god of war, was held in March.

FACT FILE

The Roman Calendar

Julius Caesar made the Roman calendar 365 days long. That is how many days our calendar has today. Many months on the new calendar were named for Roman gods. These months include January for Janus, the god of gates, and March for Mars, the god of war. Other months were named for Roman rulers. These include July for Julius Caesar and August for Augustus.

▶ The Roman calendar was created in 45 B.C. This is similar to the calendar we use today.

1. What is a republic? What is a senate?

2. Describe the different homes that people had in ancient Rome.

3. How was the calendar Julius Caesar made like the one we use today?

4. How is our government like ancient Rome's government?

5. Describe some architectural styles and materials that the ancient Romans invented.

Link to Writing

READ THINK EXPLAIN **Writing Prompt:** The civilizations of ancient Greece and Rome were alike in many ways. Think about their geography, trade, government, and culture. Then write a paragraph comparing the two civilizations.

Test Talk

Use Information from the Text

Directions: You can use details from the text to answer questions. Follow these steps.

- Read the question.
- Look for and circle key words in the question.
- Find details in the text that answer the question. **Make notes** about the details.
- Reread the question and your notes. Cross out notes that do not match the question. Add details, if needed.

Try It Write each question on a separate piece of paper. Then circle key words. Write your notes and answers using the style shown below each question. Use details from the text to support your answers.

1. Why was the war between Rome and Carthage important?

My Notes: _____

_____

_____

My Answer: _____

_____

_____

2. What role did forums play in Roman life?

My Notes: _____

_____

_____

My Answer: _____

_____

_____

Here are some projects to do on your own or in a group.

Visit A City

Write a postcard Suppose you have decided to visit one of the cities in the Roman Empire. Research the place you have chosen. You should use resources in your classroom or library. Make a postcard you might send. Draw a picture showing something about the place you have chosen. Write a note on the back of it.

Roman Roads

Make a model Form a group. Have the group work together to research more about the roads that connected the Roman Empire. Write a report about what you learned. Then draw a picture or make a model or sculpture of a Roman road to illustrate your report.

Great Zimbabwe

▶ This map is inside a bronze pendant found at Great Zimbabwe.

What remains of the ancient city of Great Zimbabwe (zihm BOB way) is today part of the country of Zimbabwe. Zimbabwe is located in southeastern Africa.

The vast plains of Zimbabwe lie to the east of the Kalahari (CAHL uh HAHR ee) Desert. A **plain** is a large area of flat land. The plains also lie between the Zambezi and Limpopo Rivers. The modern country of Zimbabwe is named after the ancient city.

The people of the ancient city planted grains and herded animals on the plains. Great Zimbabwe was near a number of rivers. However, it was not on the shores of a river

▶ The Zambezi River runs along the northern border of Zimbabwe.

▶ Many kinds of animals, including elephants, buffalo, and lions, live on the plains of Zimbabwe.

or sea. The closest ocean was the Indian Ocean. It was 250 miles away.

Yet Great Zimbabwe's location did help it grow into a wealthy city. Some of southern Africa's richest gold mines were near Great Zimbabwe. This gold was used for trade throughout Africa and Asia. Great Zimbabwe was located along a trade route. This trade route connected Great Zimbabwe to the Indian Ocean.

REVIEW How did the location of Great Zimbabwe help it to grow into a wealthy city? **Summarize**

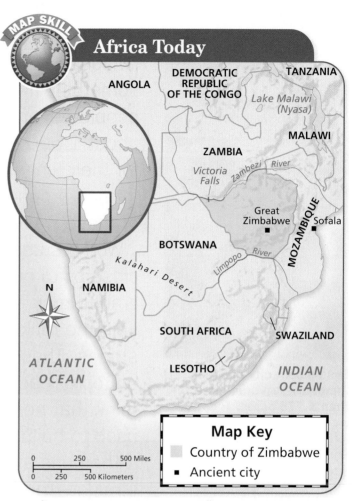

MAP SKILL

Africa Today

ANGOLA

DEMOCRATIC REPUBLIC OF THE CONGO

TANZANIA

Lake Malawi (Nyasa)

MALAWI

ZAMBIA

Victoria Falls

Zambezi River

Great Zimbabwe

MOZAMBIQUE

Sofala

BOTSWANA

Kalahari Desert

Limpopo River

NAMIBIA

N

SOUTH AFRICA

SWAZILAND

ATLANTIC OCEAN

LESOTHO

INDIAN OCEAN

0   250   500 Miles
0   250   500 Kilometers

Map Key
Country of Zimbabwe
■ Ancient city

▶ Great Zimbabwe was located in the southeastern part of Africa.

MAP SKILL Use a Map *What two rivers are closest to the location of Great Zimbabwe?*

History of Great Zimbabwe

The word *zimbabwe* comes from the Shona language. Its meaning is not clear, but it is something like "houses of stone." The Shona people began to build large stone buildings about 1,000 years ago. These buildings were for their kings. A number of walled cities formed around these buildings. The largest of these was Great Zimbabwe.

Workers used a natural resource that was close by to build their city. They gathered granite rock from the area's hills. Then they split the rock into smaller square-shaped stones. These smaller stones were stacked on top of each other. Some archaeologists think that nearly a million granite rocks were used to build Great Zimbabwe.

The huge stone buildings were built very straight. The largest part of the walled city is called the Great Enclosure. An **enclosure** is an area that has a structure around it like a wall or a fence. Parts of the Great Enclosure still exist today. It is one of the largest ancient structures in Africa.

▶ The ancient city of Great Zimbabwe covered more than 1,779 acres. Today we can still see what is left of the stone walls and the areas where huts once stood.

History of Great Zimbabwe

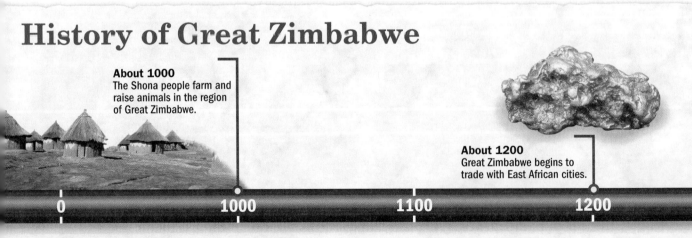

About 1000
The Shona people farm and raise animals in the region of Great Zimbabwe.

About 1200
Great Zimbabwe begins to trade with East African cities.

| 0 | 1000 | 1100 | 1200 |

People lived in the city of Great Zimbabwe for about 300 years. No one is sure why they left. Some scientists believe that the high population may have harmed the environment. It is also possible that gold traders began to use other routes. People may have followed the traders to new locations. New groups later farmed and traded in southern Africa. Some think these were the relatives of the people who live in the country of Zimbabwe today.

REVIEW What might have caused the people of Great Zimbabwe to leave the city? **Cause and Effect**

▶ **Great Zimbabwe was one of the largest and wealthiest of the ancient African cultures.**

The ruler lived inside the enclosure.

The outside wall was 16 feet thick at the bottom and 32 feet tall.

The stone tower was solid all the way through.

A v-shaped pattern decorated part of the outside wall.

1300s
The Shona people build stone walls around the city of Great Zimbabwe.

1400s
Great Zimbabwe reaches the height of its power.

About 1500
People leave Great Zimbabwe and move to other regions.

1300   1400   1500   1600

Government of Great Zimbabwe

Kings ruled Great Zimbabwe. The king lived with his guards in a building on top of the highest hill in the city. This let him see what was going on in the land below.

▶ **The king of Great Zimbabwe met with traders, priests, and other people high up on the hill.**

The queen probably lived in the Great Enclosure. All important government workers also lived there.

Many people believe that the walls of the Great Enclosure were not built for safety. Instead, they were to show the power the king had over his people. The walls also were for privacy. The royal family did not want people outside the walls to see them.

REVIEW Why would the king of Great Zimbabwe have wanted to live up on a hill? **Main Idea and Details**

FACT FILE

Rituals of the Rulers

Ancient African rulers often rose to power through ceremonies. These ceremonies and rituals made the people believe the rulers had special powers. The ceremonies set the king apart from other people. No one is certain how the kings of Great Zimbabwe became rulers. Yet it is likely that they followed the same traditions as other ancient African kings at that time.

▶ **Some African rulers wore beaded crowns such as this one.**

Economy of Great Zimbabwe

Great Zimbabwe's trade involved both cattle and gold. Herds of cattle were raised on the plains of Great Zimbabwe. The rulers of Great Zimbabwe traded the cattle for large amounts of gold. The gold came from nearby gold mines. Then the gold was traded for other items throughout Africa, Europe, and Asia.

The rulers of Great Zimbabwe grew very wealthy from trade. They used this wealth to pay many of the people who were working on the stone buildings.

▶ Other items found near Great Zimbabwe include this Chinese ink pot.

▶ Eastern African merchants used trade routes on both land and sea.

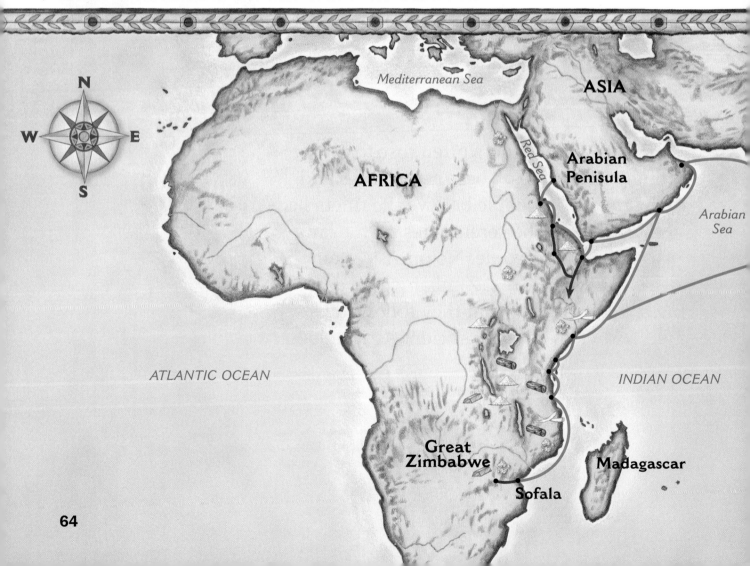

There was a sudden increase in building in the 1300s. This happened in both Great Zimbabwe and in the cities on the East African coast. Some historians think that trade between the two regions began to grow about this time.

Sofala was an important city on the East African coast. Traders carried goods from Sofala to Arabia, India, China, and further into Africa. These goods included gold and copper for beads, cloth, and pottery.

▶ Ceramic items from China are among the most common items archaeologists find in Great Zimbabwe.

REVIEW How did Great Zimbabwe's trade affect the building of the city?
Draw Conclusions

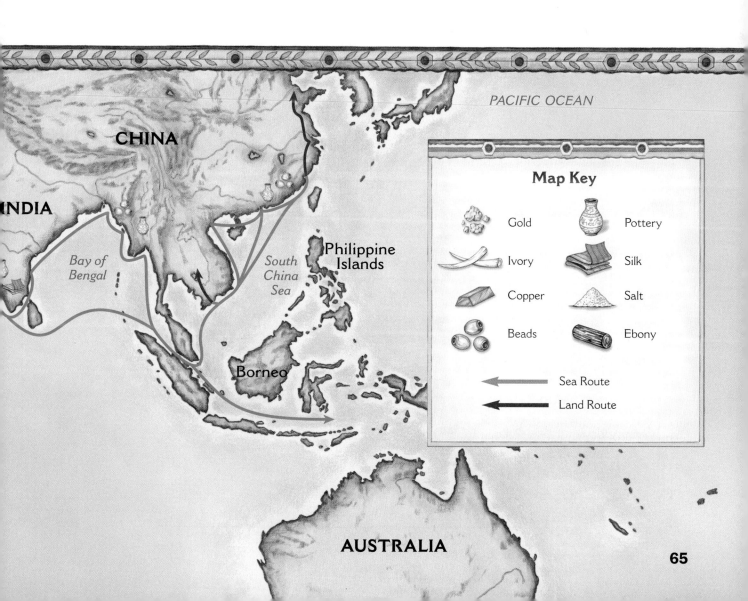

PACIFIC OCEAN

CHINA

INDIA

Bay of Bengal

South China Sea

Philippine Islands

Borneo

AUSTRALIA

Map Key

Gold

Ivory

Copper

Beads

Pottery

Silk

Salt

Ebony

Sea Route

Land Route

Map and Globe Skills

Read a Resource Map

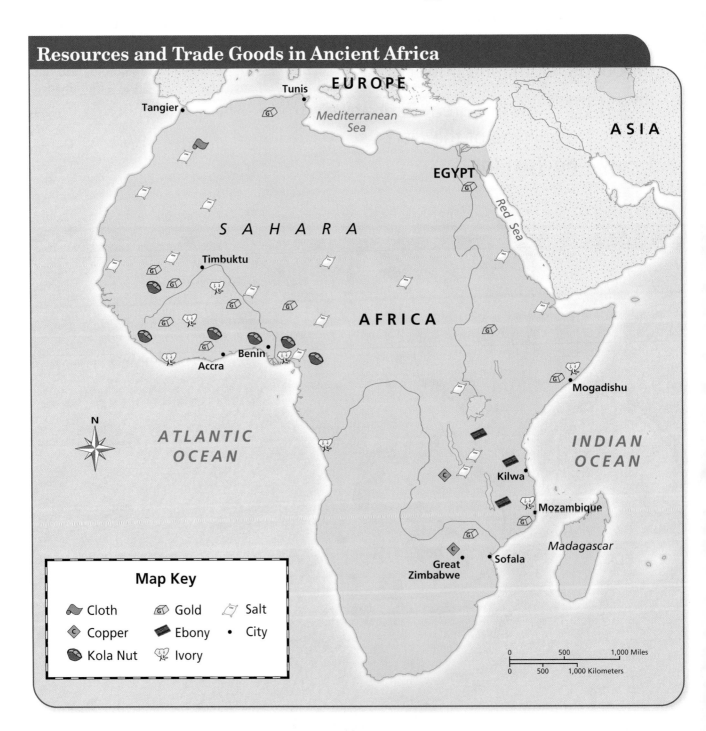

Resources and Trade Goods in Ancient Africa

EUROPE

Tunis

Tangier

Mediterranean Sea

ASIA

EGYPT

Red Sea

S A H A R A

Timbuktu

A F R I C A

Benin

Accra

N

ATLANTIC OCEAN

Mogadishu

Kilwa

INDIAN OCEAN

Mozambique

Madagascar

Great Zimbabwe

Sofala

Map Key

- Cloth
- Copper
- Kola Nut
- Gold
- Ebony
- Ivory
- Salt
- City

0   500   1,000 Miles

0   500   1,000 Kilometers

What? A **resource map** is a map that shows the natural resources and trade goods found in a region, in a country, or on a continent. A resource map also shows where these natural resources can be found. The resource map of Africa on page 66 uses symbols to show where resources and trade goods were located. Sometimes a resource map will use different colors to show where resources can be found.

Why? You have just learned about trade in and around Great Zimbabwe. Africans have traded the rich resources of their continent for hundreds of years. They trade them for goods from other places in the world. A resource map can help you understand why different places become trading centers for different types of goods.

How? Look at the map on page 66. It shows the location of resources and trade goods in Africa long ago. Look at the map key to see resources or trade goods in ancient Africa. Then locate the resources and trade goods on the map. You can see what regions of Africa were rich in particular resources.

Think and Apply

❶ Which resource or trade good did Africa have the most of?

❷ What resource or trade good did it have the least of?

❸ Name three resources or trade goods that were located near Great Zimbabwe. Then name three resources or trade goods that people in Great Zimbabwe would have had to trade with other parts of Africa to get.

Culture of Great Zimbabwe

Not a lot is known about the people of Great Zimbabwe. They had no written language. They left no records behind. All that we know about them comes from the **ruins,** or remains, of the walled city they built hundreds of years ago.

Some historians think that more than 10,000 people lived in Great Zimbabwe. Some historians think that only the richest people lived within the walled city itself. Other people would have lived in huts set close together outside the stone walls. These huts were made of a material called *daga,* which is mud mixed with plants.

▶ Birds carved out of soapstone were found in an area used for ceremonies. They may have been used as symbols for Great Zimbabwe's rulers.

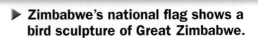

▶ Zimbabwe's national flag shows a bird sculpture of Great Zimbabwe.

Farmers grew grains in the rich soil of the area. They also raised herds of cattle, sheep, and goats. Craft workers made jugs and other clay containers. The containers were used for cooking, collecting grains, and carrying water.

People played an instrument called the mbira (em bee ra) at religious and social events and for the king. It is still played today. The mbira is the traditional musical instrument of the Shona people. It is made of metal keys attached to a wooden box. A musician plays the mbira with both thumbs plucking the keys. Traditional mbira tunes have been passed down for hundreds of years.

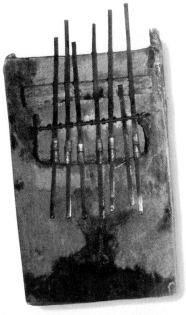

REVIEW How do we know about the people of Great Zimbabwe? **Main Idea and Details**

▶ Both traditional musicians and modern bands from Zimbabwe use the mbira.

1. What does the word *zimbabwe* mean? Why is this a good name for Great Zimbabwe?

2. On what continent is Great Zimbabwe located?

3. What natural resource did the people of Great Zimbabwe use to build their city?

4. Why was Sofala an important city to Great Zimbabwe?

5. How does mbira music keep the traditions of the Shona people alive?

Link to **Writing**

READ THINK EXPLAIN **Writing Prompt:** The ruins of Great Zimbabwe can tell us about the people who lived there. Look at the pictures of the ruins throughout this lesson. Then write a description of what you see.

Test Talk

Use Information from Graphics

Directions: You can use details from a photograph to answer a question. Follow these steps.

- Read the question.
- Look for and circle key words in the question.
- Use details from the photograph to answer the question.

Try It Write on a separate piece of paper. Circle key words. Then use information from the photographs to answer each question.

1. Based on the photograph on pages 58 and 59, describe the land where Great Zimbabwe is located.

2. Based on the photograph on page 62, describe where the king met with other people.

Do these projects on your own or in a group.

A City Design

Make a drawing Form a group. Research more about the Great Enclosure. Make a drawing of the design of the Great Enclosure. Label its many parts. Present your drawing to the rest of the class.

How Does It Sound?

Listen to music Ask your teacher how to find some recordings of mbira music. Then listen to some songs. Write two or three sentences that describe the music.

England in the Middle Ages

► A gold belt buckle from Suffolk, England

► London Bridge was built about 1,000 years ago. The bridge was crowded with houses and shops during the Middle Ages.

England is located on a large island that we know today as Great Britain. Great Britain is part of the continent of Europe. Wales lies to the west of England. Scotland is to the north. No part of England is more than 75 miles from a body of water.

For many years the English thought that the ocean was dangerous. They believed that other people could sail across it to take over England. Later, England built a strong navy. They did this for protection. They also used the sea to sail to other countries for trade.

England grew into a powerful kingdom during a time called the Middle Ages. This period lasted from about A.D. 500 to A.D. 1500. At first, people lived in small villages. Farmers

LONDON BRIDGE.

grew crops such as wheat, barley, and oats. They also raised sheep for wool. Wool was an important good. Merchants began to trade English goods for goods from other countries. Small villages grew into large towns. Towns were used as marketplaces for goods to be traded.

Towns in England became very crowded as the populations grew. Some towns, such as London, grew into cities. London is still an important trading center. It became the capital city of England.

REVIEW How did the English use the ocean to their advantage? **Cause and Effect**

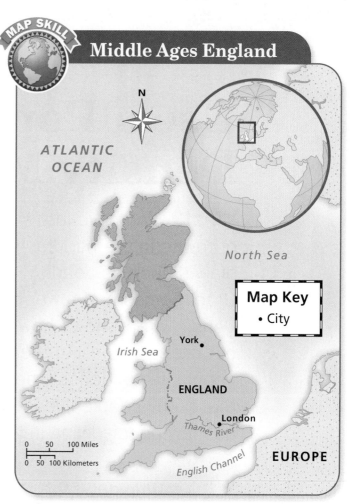

Middle Ages England

MAP SKILL

Map Key
• City

▶ In the 1300s, many towns and cities were growing in population in England.

MAP SKILL Directions *What direction would you travel to go from London to York?*

Use a Population Density Map

What? You have just read about the growth of towns in the Middle Ages. You learned that places such as London had many people. Other places had fewer people. A **population density map** shows how population is spread out over an area. An area where a lot of people live is densely populated. That means that many people live in one area. If an area has few people living in it, it is less populated.

Why? You can use a population density map to see how physical geography affects where people live. Information such as the most densely populated areas in England today is shown on the map. Less densely populated areas are also shown.

How? This map uses color to show population density. Look at the map key. The color white is at the bottom of the column with colored squares. Places on the map with this color have the least amount of people. Population increases with each color as you move up the column. Which color shows areas with the most dense population?

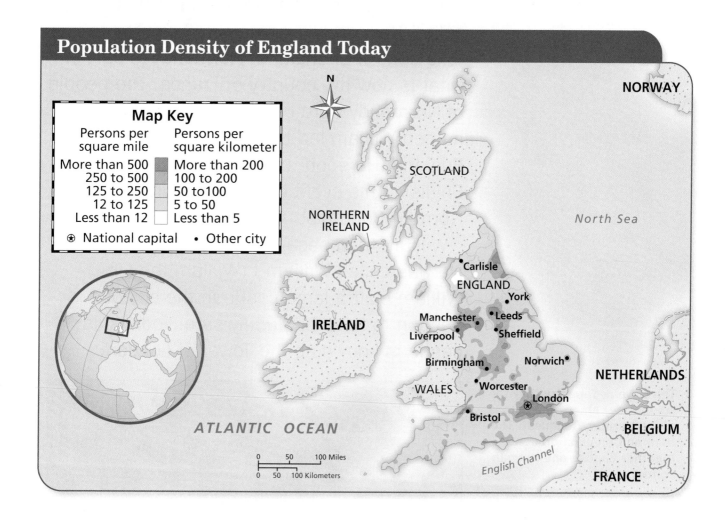

Population Density of England Today

Map Key

Persons per square mile	Persons per square kilometer
More than 500	More than 200
250 to 500	100 to 200
125 to 250	50 to 100
12 to 125	5 to 50
Less than 12	Less than 5

⊛ National capital • Other city

N

NORWAY

SCOTLAND

North Sea

NORTHERN IRELAND

Carlisle

ENGLAND

York

Manchester

Leeds

IRELAND

Liverpool

Sheffield

Birmingham

Norwich

NETHERLANDS

Worcester

WALES

London

Bristol

ATLANTIC OCEAN

BELGIUM

English Channel

FRANCE

0   50   100 Miles
0   50   100 Kilometers

Think and Apply

❶ What is a population density map?

❷ Which city has about the same population density as Norwich—Worcester or Liverpool? How do you know?

❸ Which city in England is the most densely populated? Why do you think this is so?

History of England in the Middle Ages

A group of people from a small kingdom called Normandy (NOR mun dee) wanted to take control of England. Normandy is part of what is now the country of France. The people of Normandy were called Normans. A duke named William led the Norman army into England. He soon won the war against the English. This event became known as the Norman Conquest. A **conquest** is a takeover.

William then became king of England. He was called William I (William the First). William built a large castle in the city of London to keep his family safe. Today this castle is known as the Tower of London.

▶ **The Bayeux Tapestry (bay YOO TAP es tree) shows the details of the Norman Conquest. The Norman Conquest brought together English and Norman cultures.**

History of England in the Middle Ages

About 400
The Middle Ages begin.

A.D. 400   600   800

England and France fought many small wars during the late Middle Ages. Together these became known as the Hundred Years' War. The wars really lasted 116 years. They began when the English king declared himself king of France. The English won most of the battles. But France won the war. England and France were ruled by separate kings from that point on.

REVIEW What happened after the Norman Conquest? **Sequence**

> William was crowned King of England on Christmas Day in 1066.

FACT FILE

The Domesday Book

King William I wanted a written record of his wealth. The record showed all the land in his kingdom. It also showed how many people, sheep, pigs, and other animals were living on the land. This written record became a book known as the Domesday (DOOMS day) Book. It is the oldest public record about life in England.

> The Domesday Book included a list of all the land King William I owned.

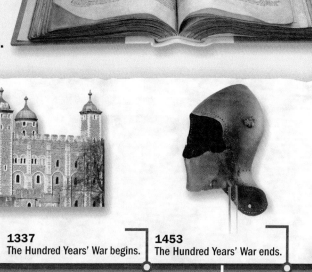

1066
Normans invade England.

1067
Work begins on the Tower of London.

1086
The Domesday Book is completed.

1337
The Hundred Years' War begins.

1453
The Hundred Years' War ends.

1000   1200   1400

Government of England in the Middle Ages

The king ruled all of England. He owned all the land. But he gave some of the land to his **lords,** or his most important nobles. In return, they promised to protect him. The lords hired soldiers to fight battles for the king. These soldiers were called **knights.**

The poorest people in England during the Middle Ages were **peasants** (PEZ ints). They did not own any land. Instead, they lived and worked on land that belonged to the lords. They produced the goods that the lords needed. In exchange, the lords gave protection to the peasants. This system was known as feudalism (FYOO dul iz um).

▶ **Knights often wore armor such as this. Boys began training to be knights at the age of seven. They would live and learn in a lord's castle.**

▶ **Lords, knights, and their families lived in castles. Castles were often dark, cold, and damp places to live.**

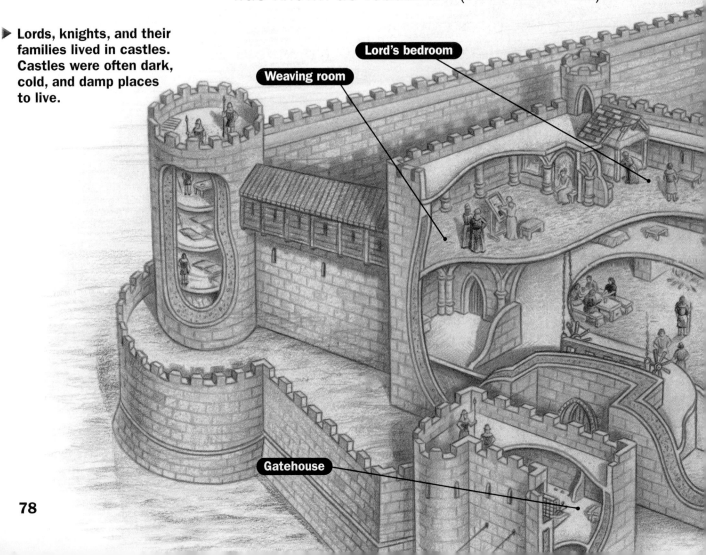

Weaving room

Lord's bedroom

Gatehouse

In 1215 a group of lords thought that the king had too much power. Together, the lords wrote up a legal document. The document was called the Magna Carta (MAG na CAR ta).

The Magna Carta said that lords had certain rights, such as the right to a fair trial. The lords forced the king to sign it. It was the first time the law was able to reduce the power of the monarchy (MAHN are key). In a **monarchy** a king or queen is the ruler.

___

REVIEW How did feudalism work?
Summarize

▶ **The Magna Carta did not give rights to all people. But it limited the power of the king for the first time.**

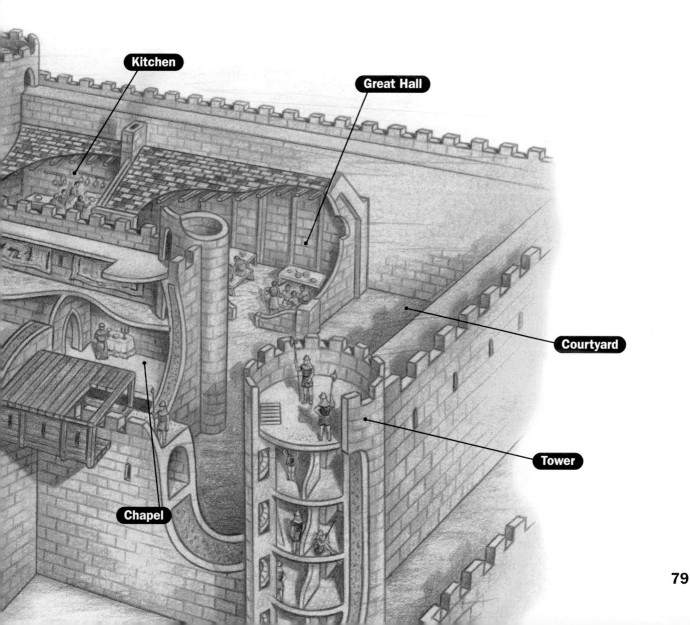

Kitchen

Great Hall

Courtyard

Tower

Chapel

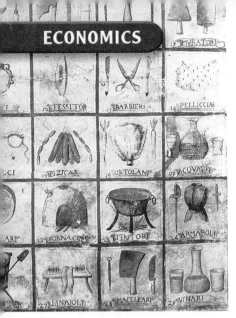

ECONOMICS

> Each guild had its own symbol. Symbols were often the tools used by the craftpeople in the guild.

Economy of England in the Middle Ages

England's most important trade item was wool. English merchants also traded coal, wood, iron, and copper. They traded these items in Europe and Asia for such things as spices, silk, olive oil, and jewelry.

Traders and craft workers who specialized in one type of product formed groups called **guilds** (GILDS). Each craft, such as carpentry, had its own guild. The guild made rules about prices and the quality of the products. People who belonged to guilds controlled trade

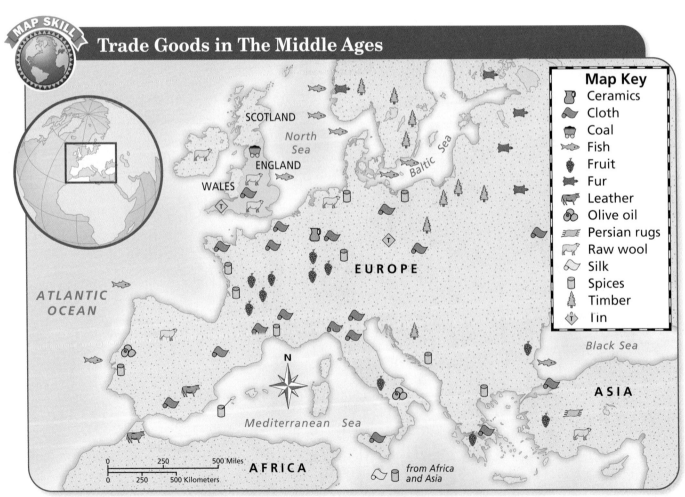

Trade Goods in The Middle Ages

Map Key
- Ceramics
- Cloth
- Coal
- Fish
- Fruit
- Fur
- Leather
- Olive oil
- Persian rugs
- Raw wool
- Silk
- Spices
- Timber
- Tin

> Trade between Europe, Asia and Africa helped people get goods they could not make or grow themselves.

MAP SKILL   Use a Map Key   *What one item can be found in Asia, Europe, and England?*

throughout England. They were often the only ones allowed to buy or sell certain products.

Large fairs were held in different cities in England and in other countries each year. Merchants from many different countries would come to these fairs. Lords would send their servants there to buy a year's supply of goods. Some people would come just to look at the new items for sale. There was usually entertainment for everyone at the fairs, including music and dancing.

REVIEW How were guilds important to the growth of trade in England in the Middle Ages? **Main Idea and Details**

▶ This is how many street scenes in the Middle Ages looked. People would buy different goods in the streets or at local fairs.

Culture of England in the Middle Ages

Few people lived in castles in the Middle Ages. Many families lived in small cottages in villages. The cottages had just one or two rooms. They were made of wood with straw roofs and dirt floors. They had stone fireplaces that were used for cooking and for heat.

Most children did some kind of work. Children of merchants helped their parents sell goods. Some boys were sent away to learn a craft or trade. Girls helped their mothers bake, raise ducks and geese, and milk cows. Most people could not read. However, families often spent time together telling and listening to stories.

Clothing in the Middle Ages was made of wool or linen. Men and boys usually wore tunics. Women and girls wore long gowns with sleeveless tunics over them.

▶ Clothing was very important during the Middle Ages. It showed a person's position in society.

▶ Musicians often entertained at fairs or feasts.

▶ **Cambridge University, in Cambridge, England, is one of the oldest universities in Europe.**

Every English village had a church. The church was very important to daily life. There were also special places for men and women to go to study religion. Men known as monks lived in communities called monasteries. Women called nuns lived in convents. They spent their whole lives in these communities.

New types of schools began by the late Middle Ages. These schools taught subjects such as medicine and law. They became the first universities.

REVIEW How was life in England during the Middle Ages alike and different for boys and girls? **Compare and Contrast**

1. Copy the chart below on a separate piece of paper. Compare and contrast life for the lords and life for the peasants in England during the Middle Ages.

Compare/Alike	Contrast/Different

2. How did guilds control trade?

3. What effect did the Magna Carta have on the power of the king of England?

4. Why were fairs such an important part of economic life in England during the Middle Ages?

5. What can the Domesday Book teach us about life in England during the Middle Ages?

Link to Writing

READ THINK EXPLAIN **Writing Prompt:** The city of London was a crowded and busy place in the Middle Ages. Suppose you were a visitor to London during that time. Write a journal entry describing what you might see.

 Test Talk

Write Your Answer to Score High

Directions: A question may tell you to write an answer. Follow these steps to make sure your answer is correct, complete, and focused.

- Read the question.
- Make notes about details that answer the question.
- Reread the question and your notes. Add details, if needed.
- Use details from your notes to answer the question.
- Check your answer. Ask yourself:
  — Is my answer correct, complete, and focused?
  — Do all my details help answer the question?

Try It Copy Patti's notes and answer on a separate piece of paper. Add details to her notes, if necessary. Write to explain what she needs to do to score higher.

1. What was the importance of the Hundred Years' War? Use details from the text to support your answer.

Patti's Notes:

wars between England and France, really lasted more than 100 years; France won the war

Patti's Answer:

England and France fought the Hundred Years' War. It really lasted more than 100 years. France was the winner.

To score higher, what does Patti need to do?

Here are some projects you can do on your own or in a group.

Life in an English Castle

Create a model Form a group. Research more about English castles in the Middle Ages. Make a scene showing part of a castle. Share your model with the class.

An Event in English History

Make a mural Form a group. Choose an event that happened in England in the Middle Ages. You might be interested in one you have already read about. You might want to research some other event. Work with your group to create a mural that shows scenes from this event.

Index

Titles appear in italics. An *m* in front of a page number indicates a map.
A *p* in front of a page number indicates a picture.

Credits

MAPS
MapQuest.com, Inc.

ILLUSTRATIONS
2, 54 Neal Armstrong
4 Ralph Voltz
10, 24 Geoff McCormack
12 William Graham
34 Andy Zito
38, 40, 53, 61 Robert Lawson
64 Susan J. Carlson
78 Tony Crnkovich
81 Tom Metcalf
82 Dennis Soderstrom

PHOTOGRAPHS
Every effort has been made to secure permission and provide appropriate credit for photographic material. The publisher deeply regrets any omission and pledges to correct errors called to its attention in subsequent editions.

Unless otherwise acknowledged, all photographs are the property of Scott Foresman, a division of Pearson Education.

Photo locators denoted as follows: Top (T), Center (C), Bottom (B), Left (L), Right (R), Background (Bkgd)

Cover
(Bkgd) ©Explorer, Paris/SuperStock, (C) ©Egyptian National Museum, Cairo, Egypt/SuperStock, (BR) Musee du Louvre, Paris/Dagli Orti/The Art Archive, (TL) British Museum/©Dorling Kindersley, (TLC) Victoria and Albert Museum, London/Art Resource, NY, (TCL) ©Jan Vinchon Numismatist Paris/Dagli Orti/The Art Archive, (TCR) The Granger Collection, (TRC) British Museum/Eileen Tweedy/The Art Archive, (TR) ©North Carolina Museum of Art/Corbis

Front Matter
vii ©Photowood Inc./Corbis
2 ©Egyptian Museum Cairo/Dagli Orti/The Art Archive
4 (TL) ©RogerWood/Corbis, (BL) Egyptian Museum Turin/Dagli Orti/The Art Archive, (BR) ©Réunion des Musées Nationaux/Art Resource, NY
5 (BC) ©Robert Frerck/Odyssey/Chicago, (BR) ©Pictor International/ ImageState/Alamy.com, (BR) The Granger Collection, (BC) ©Hugh Sitton/Getty Images, (CR) Boltin Picture Library, (TR) Art Resource, NY
6 ©Egyptian National Museum, Cairo, Egypt/SuperStock
8 (TL) ©Sami Sarkis/Alamy.com, (B) ©Fotos and Photos/Index Stock Imagery
9 ©Egyptian Museum Cairo/The Art Archive

Unit 1
10 (TL) ©Dorling Kindersley, (BR) ©M. Clave/Jacana/Photo Researchers, Inc., (BR) ©Leslie Garland/LGPL/Alamy.com, (BR) ©Russ Lappa/Science Source/Photo Researchers, Inc.
11 (TR) ©Christine Osborne/Worldwide Picture Library/Alamy.com, (BR) The Granger Collection
12 ©Egyptian Museum Turin/Dagli Orti/The Art Archive
13 (TR) ©Dagli Orti/The Art Archive, (B) John Woodcock/©Dorling Kindersley
15 ©Gianni Dagli Orti/Corbis

Unit 2
16 (TL) British Museum/©Dorling Kindersley, (BL) ©Macduff Everton/Corbis, (B) Keren Su/China Span
17 Musée Guimet Paris/The Art Archive
20 (CR) ©Royal Ontario Museum/Corbis, (BC) ©Asian Art & Archaeology, Inc./Corbis, (BL) ©Asian Art & Archaeology, Inc./Corbis, (BR) H. Rogers/Art Directors & TRIP Photo Library
21 (TR) ChinaStock, (CL) ©Dennis Cox/ChinaStock, (BC) ©Paul Freeman/Bridgeman Art Library, (BR) British Library/©Dorling Kindersley, (CR) British Museum/©Dorling Kindersley
22 (B) Keren Su/China Span, (TL) The British Library/Art Archive
24 (TL) The Granger Collection, (CR) ©Giraudon/Art Resource, NY, (CL) ©Robert Holmes/Corbis
25 (TL) Dagli Orti (A)/The Art Archive, (BR) ©Bettmann/Corbis
26 (TL) The Granger Collection, (CL) ©Liu Liqun/Corbis, (BR) ©Dorling Kindersley
27 (B) ©Kevin Fleming/Corbis, (TR) ©Charles Walker/Topfoto/The Image Works, Inc., (CL) ©Réunion des Musées Nationaux/Art Resource, NY

Unit 3
30 ©David Lees/Corbis
31 (TR) ©Sheldan Collins/Corbis, (B) Getty Images
32 (TL) ©Chiaramonti Museum Vatican/Dagli Orti (A)/The Art Archive, (BL) ©Archaeological Museum Mykonos/Dagli Orti/The Art Archive, (BC) ©Dave Bartruff/Corbis
33 (TR) Corbis, (CR) ©Mick Roessler/Index Stock Imagery, (BL) Antonio M. Rosario/Image Bank, (BR) ©Araldo de Luca/Corbis
34 ©Gianni Dagli Orti/Corbis
35 (TR) ©Gianni Dagli Orti/Corbis, (CR) ©Wolfgang Kaehler/Corbis
37 ©Jon Davison/Lonely Planet Images
38 ©Gianni Dagli Orti/Corbis
39 ©Gail Mooney/Corbis
40 British Museum/©Dorling Kindersley
41 ©Scala/Art Resource, NY

Unit 4
44 Provinciaal Museum, G. M. Kam Nijmegen, Netherlands/Dagli Orti/The Art Archive, ©Bettmann/Corbis
45 ©Hilbich/AKG London Ltd.
46 (CL) ©Museo di Villa Giulia Rome/Dagli Orti/The Art Archive, (CR) Vega/FPG International LLC, (BC) ©Massimo Mastrorillo/Corbis
47 (C) ©Dagli Orti/The Art Archive, (BR) ©Alinari/Art Resource, NY, (BC) The Granger Collection
48 (TL) ©Scala/Art Resource, NY, (BL) ©Pixtal/SuperStock, (BC) ©Museo della Civilta Romana Rome/Dagli Orti/The Art Archive, (BR) ©Scala/Art Resource, NY
49 (TL) ©Museo Capitolino, Rome, Italy/ET Archive, London/SuperStock, (BR) ©Roger Ressmeyer/Corbis
50 (TL) ©Pirozzi/AKG London Ltd., (B) Scala/Art Resource, NY
51 ©Alinari/Art Resource, NY
52 (TL) ©Jan Vinchon Numismatist Paris/Dagli Orti/The Art Archive, (BL) ©Scala/Art Resource, NY
53 Corbis
54 Corbis
55 (CR) ©Bettmann/Corbis, (BR) Ancient Art & Architecture Collection Ltd.

Unit 5
58 (TL) Darrel Plowes, (B) ©Dennis Johnson/Lonely Planet Images, (BL) ©Joe Mann/Lonely Planet Images
60 (BR) Max Alexander/©Dorling Kindersley, (TL) ©David Wall/Lonely Planet Images, (BL) ©Frank Perkins/Index Stock Imagery
61 (BR) Darrel Plowes, (BL) ©Colin Hoskins; Cordaiy Photo Library Ltd./Corbis
62 Jason Laure/Woodfin Camp & Associates
63 The British Museum/The Image Works, Inc.
64 Darrel Plowes
65 Darrel Plowes
68 (CL) Heini Schneebeli/Bridgeman Art Library, (BR) Dream Maker Software
69 (TR) ©H Rogers/Art Directors & TRIP Photo Library, (B) Vincent Talbot/Lonely Planet Images

Unit 6
72 (TL) ©British Museum/Topham/Corbis, (B) Peter Adamas/Alamy.com, (BL) Mary Evans Picture Library
76 (BL) ©The British Museum/Topham-HIP/The Image Works, Inc., (C) ©Giraudon/Art Resource, NY
77 (CR) ©Hulton Archive/Getty Images, (CR) ©Michael Freeman/Corbis, (BL) ©Musee de la Reine, Bayeux France/Bridgeman Art Library, (BC) ©Marcin Libera/Alamy.com, (BR) ©The British Museum/Topham-HIP/The Image Works, Inc.
78 ©Dorling Kindersley
79 ©Bettmann/Corbis
80 ©Duomo, Orvieto, Umbria, Italy/Roger-Viollet, Paris/Bridgeman Art Library International Ltd.
82 Mary Evans Picture Library
83 ©Michael Nicholson/Corbis
115 ©Dallas and John Heaton/Corbis